an INTEGRATED APPROACH *to* LEARNING

HEINEMANN
Portsmouth, NH

Lorraine Wilson
with David Malmgren,
Shirl Ramage and
Leanne Schulz

Contents

HEINEMANN EDUCATIONAL BOOKS, INC.
361 Hanover Street, Portsmouth, NH 03801-3959
Offices and agents throughout the world

First published in the USA in 1993 by Heinemann

First published in 1991 in Australia by
Thomas Nelson Australia
102 Dodds Street
South Melbourne 3205

ISBN 0 435 08786 X

Designed and typeset by Keith Lucas Design
Cover design by Karen Harbour
Printed in Hong Kong

Preface

We set out to write about integrated curriculum and specifically about the link between language and learning. Now when we read our manuscript it is evident that we are describing the learning program at one school, Moonee Ponds West. However, that is where we all work, so in one sense our manuscript can't help but be parochial. We hope, though, that our text has application for teachers everywhere.

We are grateful that in the preparation of this manuscript Di Bicknel, June Fleming and Julie Hamston agreed to be critical friends.

You Call This School!

You call this school
. . . lounging in arm chairs.
. . . being allowed to sit
where we like.
. . . a jungle of children's work hanging about
on strings.

You call this school
. . . calling teachers by first names or
even initials
. . . the Class Committee discussing ideas
proposed by the grade.
. . . talking to Frank our principal, about issues
raised by children.

You call this school
. . . writing original stories on our own topics.
. . . Answering CRAZY questions like
what is love?
why did the convict smile?
beauty is?
. . . having F.A.T. (free activity time)

You call this school
. . . having freedom of choice.
. . . being trusted.
. . . being given responsibilities
organising events
(billy cart grand prix
easter games
the mini show
and more)

You call this school
. . . reading books at our own pace
talking about them
choosing our own activities
. . . personal maths
writing, talking and finding out about
things like time
money
probability.

You call this school
. . . you might not BUT we definitely do!!!!

JOANNE GHIOCAS
MICHELLE BOTTERILL
Grade 6

Chapter 1 The integrated curriculum: Planning for learning

If language is learned best and easiest when it is whole and in natural context, then integration is a key principle for language development and learning through language. In fact language development and content become a dual curriculum. For learners it's a single curriculum focusing on what is being learned, what language is used for. But for teachers there is always a double agenda: to maximise opportunities for pupils to engage in authentic speech and literacy events while they study their community, do a literature unit on Lloyd Alexander, carry out a scientific study of mice, or develop a sense of fractions and decimals. Speaking, listening, writing and reading are all happening in context of the exploration of the world of things, events, ideas and experiences.

The content curriculum draws on the interests and experiences children have outside of school, and this incorporates the full range of oral and written functions. It becomes a broad, rich curriculum that starts where the learners are in language and knowledge and builds out from there.

Kenneth Goodman [1]

Daniel, aged 11 years, has been nominated for the Children's Council. The Council is to be a voice for the children to the principal or to the senior governing body of the school, the School Council. Daniel has designed and displayed a political poster promoting his candidacy, and as well is handing out 'How to Vote' slips, which he has written.

While Daniel has focused on some current issues in his poster, Michelle — another candidate — is promoting her personal attributes. Max, meanwhile, experiments with some standover tactics.

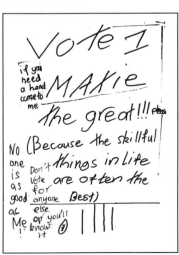

These children are using language in meaningful context. They are pleased to have been nominated for Council and would all like to be elected, but that won't be possible as there are more nominations than positions. Meanwhile, they are talking and writing to persuade, to argue, to win support for the elections, and in doing so they are learning much about democratic election procedures.

Language learning occurs when it is whole and in natural context. Daniel, Michelle and Max are using language for meaningful purpose in the context of an election.

The integrated curriculum is concerned with learning being both authentic and relevant to the children. The contexts for language use are drawn from the children's worlds outside school and from shared events and investigations initiated in the classroom. To ensure relevancy in the classroom investigations or integrated learning units, the children are involved in the selection of units and in helping to plan the body of the units. Initially they are challenged to establish their existing knowledge, and they are invited also to list those things they want to find out.

Authenticity in the program arises from the activities being for some real-life purpose: to find answers to children's questions, to seek support in an election they want to win, to write a script that will actually be performed at the school revue.

An integrated curriculum is one in which teachers plan for children to learn language at the same time they are learning something else. The 'something else' may be science or social studies, planning the school camp or writing an agenda for the Monday assembly. Language learning cannot happen in a vacuum; it is always context-bound.

Shirl and David's Grade 5-6 children were helping to plan a school camp to be held at Cave Hill Creek, out of Beaufort. In pre-camp activities in the classroom, the children were sharing their expectations for the forthcoming camp. The issue of loss of sleep arose — questions about sharing huts, talking after lights out, pillow fights. It was decided that both the children who went on camp and those not going would keep records of the actual hours slept each night; this meant that after the camp there would be recorded data from which sleeping patterns could be accurately compared. This activity was beneficial in another way: it brought together camp children and non-camp children as they worked on a common interest.

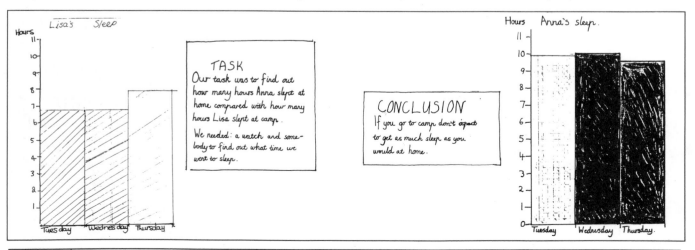

While on the camp at Cave Hill Creek, these city children were all agog when they saw the size of the eucalyptus trees. How big were the trees? Could the children work out ways of measuring them?

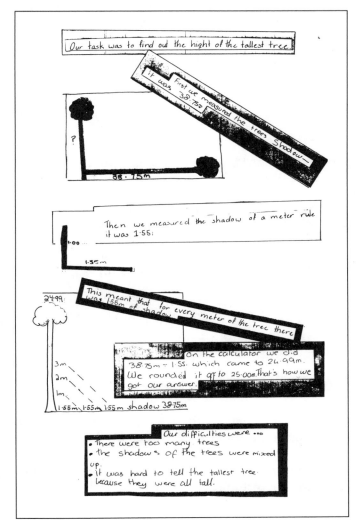

To solve these camp-related problems, the children were using language and maths: at the same time they were *learning* language and maths.

The contexts for learning

The contexts for learning — and so the contexts for learning language — may be found in any curriculum area. They may arise out of school routines or social events. They may occur in or outside school. All these contexts may be classified as either relating solely to individual children (these we are calling 'personal') or relating to groups of children (these we are calling 'shared'). Some examples from each context are given here, but the subject is explored further in chapters 3, 4 and 5.

The personal context

Each day in the classroom some children will be investigating and working through personal interests or concerns. When they are doing this, the matter under investigation will at any particular moment be of interest to only the child who is involved.

Heidi, a Grade 6 child, was quite ill with several bad bouts of the flu and missed several weeks of school. In personal writing time, Heidi chose to express her thoughts about her illness.

The Flu

You know something I don't like it's the Flu, I had it twice this year! I think it's trying to spite me. It seems whenever we are doing something good at school or Shirl's away for the week, (Ha!Ha!) I have to catch the Flu! It's terrible having to blow your nose every second of the day and your throat feels like it's got an insect in it trying to get out. And just when your feeling a bit better you watch T.V. and your Mum says "DO THE HOUSE-WORK!" **I HATE THE FLU!** I'm going to get it back somehow.

Heidi Raouf

The children write in their letter-diaries about a wide range of issues, and often these matters are quite personal. (See Appendix 2 for example of letter-diary procedure.)

Karri, aged 8 years, wrote to her teacher sharing her excitement about a forthcoming special treat for her birthday.

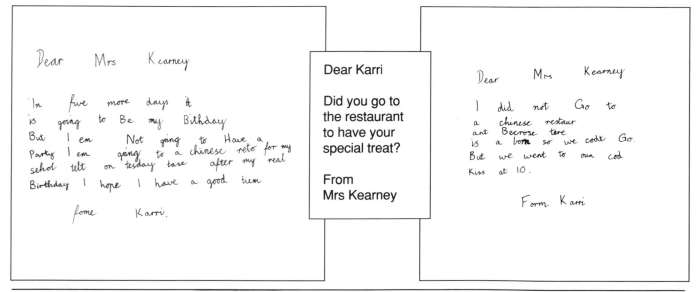

Dear Mrs Kearney

In five more days it is going to Be my Bithday But I em Not going to Have a Party I em going to a chinese reto for my sehol telt on tesday tase after my real Birthday I hope I have a good tiem

fome Karri.

Dear Karri

Did you go to the restaurant to have your special treat?

From
Mrs Kearney

Dear Mrs Kearney

I did not Go to a chinese restaurant Beerose tere is a born so we codt Go. But we went to oun cod Kiss at 10.

Form Karri

Shared contexts

School routines and special events

One example of shared context is the children's planning for, participation in and evaluation of school routines and events such as school assemblies, school concerts, school camps, billycart days, money-raising events and the junior school council.

As part of the preparation for the formation of the junior school council, teachers and children listed the sorts of issues the council might first discuss and then follow with recommendations to either the principal or the School Council. This is the combined list of issues from the children of Shirl and David's grade.

Literature choice
Method of coming to school (bikes)
Access to shop at school times
Excursions
Punishment
What we learn, how we learn
Playground equipment, sports equipment
Camp
Method of entering school (music, bell)
Office duties (answering telephone, how chosen, how long)
Playground areas
Subjects (different languages, swimming)
Lunches (canteen)
Sport options
Music (instrumental choices, longer lessons)
Hours of school (break times)
Sex education
Homework
Intraschool activities (dress-up days)

After this whole-group session, children were asked individually or in small groups to write some thoughts about one or two of the issues which particularly interested them. The idea was that when the council was formed, some of the children might have issues ready to present.

Peppe, Daniel and Bruno:

Canteen:
We could turn the dental unit into a canteen and the mothers' club could organise it.

Nancy and Sabrina:

Subjects.
More music lessons, so we can learn more and it's more than 15 minutes.

Maths should be after lunch because at the morning the people don't like it because they're asleep.

Library should be changed in different ways like no sitting down on the floor for more than 20 minutes.

PE sessions should be twice a week so you can learn different sports.

Integrated learning units

The integrated learning units, carefully planned to develop children's understandings of their physical and social worlds, give rise to many shared contexts in which children together learn, and learn language. In saying this we do not mean that all children who take part in a particular experience will necessarily learn the same things, but rather that having engaged in the one excursion or science experiment, several children will have a focus for talking together, learning together, and developing further their individual understandings.

As part of an integrated unit on the European settlement of Australia, some Grade 5-6 children in an argumentative language session listed arguments for and against the following proposition:

'People found guilty before our courts today should be deported from Australia.'

Working in groups of four, the children came up with the following arguments.

For
- By deporting criminals this may reduce crime.
- By deporting criminals our jails wouldn't be so overcrowded.
- Our criminals could be used to work in underprivileged countries, e.g. Ethiopia, to help plant crops.
- People would be scared to rob banks if they knew that if they were caught they would be sent from Australia.
- If it was done in the eighteenth century, why not do it now?
- If criminals were deported, Australia would be a safer place to live.

Against
- There may be some innocent people who the court found guilty. It would be unfair to deport them.
- There would be no guarantee that the guilty people would stop committing crimes.
- Criminals would miss their families.
- Jails in other countries would become overcrowded if Australia sent criminals there.
- Some criminals wouldn't care if they were deported. They would keep on committing crime.
- It would cost lots of money to transport criminals.
- Australia's population would decrease. We need our population to increase.

The children then met in a whole-group circle to further support or reject these arguments.

Contexts for language learning may arise from the need or interest of one child or from the shared concern or interest of a group. Planning in our classrooms must support both of these contexts.

When planning for language learning in school, teachers do not need to seek out special language content or to plan language themes. Children learn language as they learn to make friends, as they learn science and maths, as they learn about their communities, their families and themselves.

A popular conception of the integrated curriculum is that it occurs when there are integrated units such as 'Space' or 'Environment'. However, the integrated curriculum is more than the integrated unit. It is language and learning and living all inextricably intertwined, and occurring throughout the school day.

Here is one further example of children learning in a shared context. Some of the Grade 5-6 children decided to investigate a problem posed in a maths Activity Book.[2] The problem was to find out how many children could stand shoulder to shoulder in their classroom. Notice, in the two examples included here, how differently two groups approached the same problem and how much predicting, planning, reasoning and even arguing occurred as the children set about their tasks.

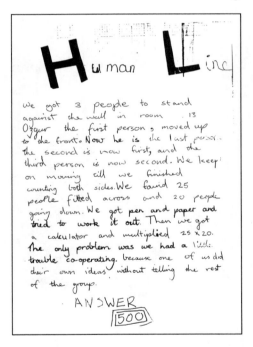

Human Line

We got 3 people to stand against the wall in room 13. Ozgur the first person, moved up to the front. Now he is the last person, the second is now first, and the third person is now second. We keep on moving till we finished counting both sides. We found 25 people fitted across and 20 people going down. We got pen and paper and tried to work it out. Then we got a calculator and multiplied 25 x 20. The only problem was we had a little trouble co-operating, because one of us did their own ideas without telling the rest of the group.

ANSWER
500

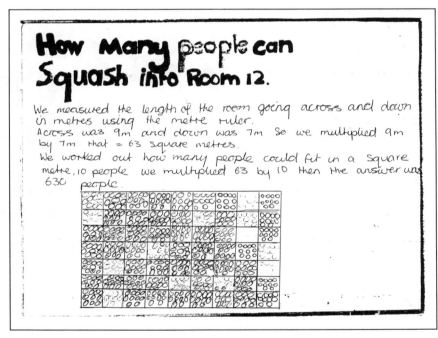

How Many people can Squash into Room 12.

We measured the length of the room going across and down in metres using the metre ruler.
Across was 9m and down was 7m so we multiplied 9m by 7m that = 63 square metres.
We worked out how many people could fit in a square metre, 10 people we multiplied 63 by 10 then the answer was 630 people.

Grade 5–6 students perform Readers Theatre for their classmates

An Integrated Approach to Learning

Chapter 2 The integrated curriculum: Planning for language development

When learning to talk, learner talkers are left to decide (take responsibility for) which particular convention or set of conventions they will attend to and subsequently internalise in their repertoires. Their 'tutors' don't try to sequence what the learner should learn.

Brian Cambourne [3]

When children are learning to speak, parents do not have a Year 1-5 'Talking Curriculum' which prescribes the items of vocabulary or speech conventions they will practise, for example, in Week 1, Month 2 or Year 3. As Cambourne says, preschool children themselves take responsibility for the order in which such speech conventions are learned and the time at which they are learned.

Therefore, when applying natural learning theory in classrooms for the development of language there is no need to break reading and writing study into small pieces and sequence them within age levels. There is no need to write a Grade 1 Spelling Curriculum or a Grade 5 Grammar Program.

This question then arises: if we take away grade-sequenced language programs, what is there to support teachers in their planning for children's continuing language development? Is there a framework or scaffold that will support teachers in their planning, thus ensuring a cohesive approach from Prep to Grade 6, and which will provide some parameters for the P–6 language curriculum yet at the same time allow children to take responsibility for the learning of language conventions?

In our planning we are supported by a three-part scaffold, the three parts being the purposes, the forms and the audiences for language. As was said in chapter 1, the content of the curriculum comes both from the children's personal experiences and the shared experiences and contexts planned by teachers. This may be summarised by the diagram on page 11.

The three-part scaffold

Language purposes

To plan for pupils using language for authentic purposes, teachers need to be familiar with the range of language purposes.

One classification of the uses of language by young children was developed by Joan Tough, and is reproduced here.[4]

1. Self-maintaining
   Strategies
   1. Referring to physical and psychological needs and wants.
   2. Protecting the self and self-interests.
   3. Justifying behaviour or claims.
   4. Criticising others.
   5. Threatening others.

2. Directing
   Strategies
   1. Monitoring own actions.
   2. Directing the actions of the self.
   3. Directing the actions of others.
   4. Collaborating in action with others.

3. Reporting on present and past experiences
   Strategies
   1. Labelling the components of the scene.
   2. Referring to detail (e.g. size, colour and other attributes).
   3. Referring to incidents.
   4. Referring to the sequence of events.
   5. Making comparisons.
   6. Recognising related aspects.
   7. Making an analysis using several of the features above.
   8. Extracting or recognising the central meaning.
   9. Reflecting on the meaning of experiences, including own feelings.

4. Towards logical reasoning
   Strategies
   1. Explaining a process.
   2. Recognising causal and dependent relationships.
   3. Recognising problems and their solutions.
   4. Justifying judgments and actions.
   5. Reflecting on events and drawing conclusions.
   6. Recognising principles.

5. Predicting
   Strategies
   1. Anticipating and forecasting events.
   2. Anticipating the detail of events.
   3. Anticipating a sequence of events.
   4. Anticipating problems and possible solutions.
   5. Anticipating and recognising alternative courses of action.
   6. Predicting the consequences of actions or events.

6. Projecting
   Strategies
   1. Projecting into the experiences of others.
   2. Projecting into the feelings of others.
   3. Projecting into the reactions of others.
   4. Projecting into situations never experienced.

7. Imagining
   Strategies
   1. Developing an imaginary situation based on real life.
   2. Developing an imaginary situation based on fantasy.
   3. Developing an original story.

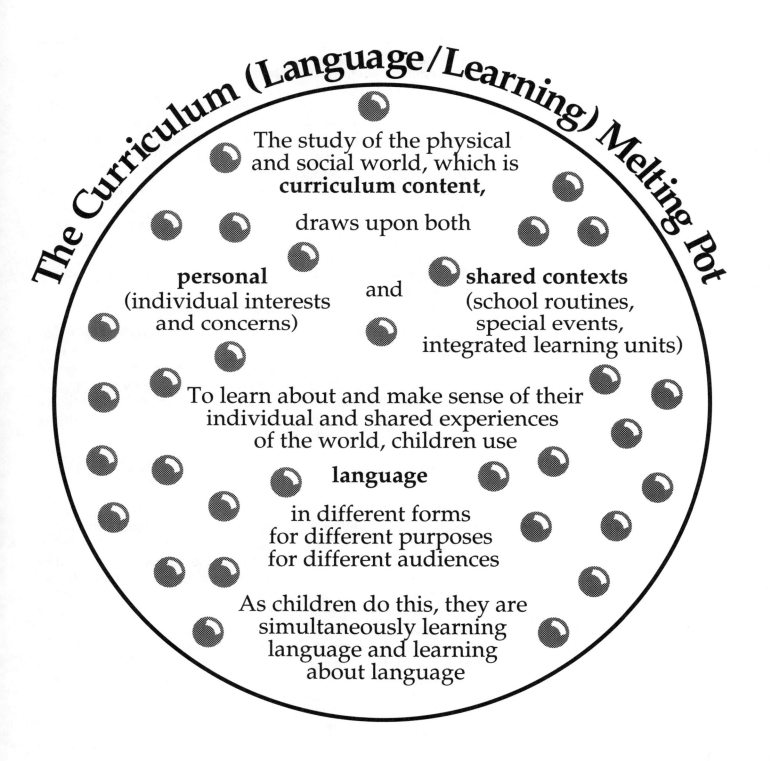

The Curriculum (Language/Learning) Melting Pot

The study of the physical and social world, which is **curriculum content,**

draws upon both

personal (individual interests and concerns)

and

shared contexts (school routines, special events, integrated learning units)

To learn about and make sense of their individual and shared experiences of the world, children use

language

in different forms for different purposes for different audiences

As children do this, they are simultaneously learning language and learning about language

Tough's classification is incomplete, since it results from a study of the way *young children* use language. Frank Smith developed the following classification of language uses or purposes which is applicable to people of all ages.[5]

1. *Instrumental*: 'I want' (language as a means of getting things, satisfying material needs).
2. *Regulatory*: 'Do as I tell you' (controlling the behaviour, feelings or attitudes of others).
3. *Interactional*: 'Me and you' (getting along with others, establishing relative status; also 'Me against you', establishing separateness).
4. *Personal*: 'Here I come' (expressing individuality, awareness of self, pride, pleasure, anger, grief).
5. *Heuristic*: 'Tell me why?' (seeking and testing knowledge).
6. *Imaginative*: 'Let's pretend' (creating new worlds, making up stories, poems).
7. *Representational*: 'I've got something to tell you' (communicating information, descriptions, expressing propositions).
8. *Divertive*: 'Enjoy this' (puns, jokes, riddles).
9. *Authoritative/contractual*: 'How it must be' (statutes, laws, regulations, arguments, contracts).
10. *Perpetuating*: 'How it was' (records, histories, diaries, notes, scores).

Being familiar with the possible different uses of language enables teachers to better evaluate both how their children are using language and the extent to which their program provides opportunity for the full range of language use. It has alerted us to the quantity of language for reporting we at one time required in our teaching, and in comparison how little we required language to project, to reason logically and to entertain. Following are illustrations from our classrooms of these three language uses.

Using language to project

Press conference

After reading a book, children prepare for a press conference. (Procedure for this activity is given in Appendix 2.) Most of them, representing ladies and gentlemen of the press, list two or three questions which they would like to ask the honoured guests—that is, two or three of the book characters. Simultaneously, several children who have volunteered to be the book characters predict questions they might be asked and practise how they might answer them.

This activity is a great way of having the children *ask* questions after reading a book rather than *answering* questions asked by the teacher. It is also a good way of developing their questioning techniques. For example, the guests at the press conference were instructed to answer questions, if they could, with 'Yes' or 'No' only, and not to give away other information; consequently, the child who asked 'Was it hard to train the animals?' in the lesson referred to below was a little agitated when he received just 'No' for an answer. That same child came back later with 'How did you train the animals?'

Here are the questions some Grade 2-3 children asked of Grandma, from *My Grandma Lived in Gooligulch*, by Graeme Base.

Was it hard to train the animals?
Was it bumpy riding on the kangaroo?
How was it in the pelican's beak?
How did you train the animals?
How high did you fly?
Have you gone near the water since?

Story retelling

Grade 5–6 girls and boys were asked to rewrite 'Cinderella' from the point of view of one of the story characters. Here are two characters' versions.

The Stepmother
I married a gullible old barron .....it only took me days to get him under my thumb. There was only one snag – his nasty little brat Cinderella! But my lovely, sweet, beautiful, little angels set her to work immediately. Ha! Ha! The handsome Prince was looking for a maiden to marry but of course my own daughters would charm him out of his socks! (Correction gold, embroidered cavalier boots!)

The King
It was so romantic to see my handsome son marry such a beautiful girl. Its really nice to see them so happy all the time – for he spent a lot of time finding the right woman. I cant stop thinking of how my son danced all night long with Cinderella at the ball.

These activities, which require the children to project into the experiences and feelings of others, are not taken for the sole purpose of having them use language to project. What happens when children do use language in this way is that they develop far greater understanding of those other people. They are better able to understand why they do what they do.

Using language towards logical reasoning

Through trial and error and listening to the children's evaluation, the following format has been devised for an argumentative language session (see also 'Argumentative language' in Appendix 2).

- The children are given a written statement, which they discuss in small groups of no more than four members. One group member acts as a scribe and lists both the supporting and the opposing arguments offered. The statement discussed may relate to a shared classroom interest or may be suggested by an individual child; for example, 'Smoking should be banned'.

- After 20 minutes of small-group pooling of arguments, the children pull their chairs into a circle. The teacher sits in the circle with them, and one child acts as chairperson in the discussion that follows. The role of the chairperson is to invite reporters to put forward their groups' arguments, to then invite speakers from the circle to support or oppose those arguments, to curb the domineering child and to encourage non-contributors to contribute.

The children thoroughly enjoy these sessions and many can now move from speaking for the proposition to speaking against it, whereas during the initial sessions they stuck defensively to their opinions.

No winners are announced, no points are scored. The children know that these sessions are for the purpose of exercising their thinking powers and enabling them better to see both sides of an argument, all in the context of confronting real-life issues.

Using language for fun (Smith's divertive purpose)

Using language for fun or to entertain involves an audience. In class publishing programs, children can write and publish humorous material for others to read. As well, a regular classroom concert or revue can provide an opportunity for them to entertain others. A regular feature of David and Shirl's Grade 5-6 program is the Revue, held at the end of each semester. It is the responsibility of those children who wish to perform in the Revue to come up with an act, script it, rehearse it, and gather the necessary props and costumes. They can seek teacher assistance if they wish, but the final responsibility for having the act ready is theirs. When the Revues were first introduced, about four years ago, many of the acts consisted of small groups of children miming pop records; now there is evidence of much greater diversity and creativity. Many groups write playscripts or TV advertisements; last Christmas three girls read and mimed some of Alan Ahlberg's poems.

For the December Revue one group wrote a parody of 'Jack and the Beanstalk' in the form of a play. Of course, the giant was the good guy and Jack was the villain. The giant plants the vegetables — namely, carrots.

Here is an extract from Scene 3.

Scene 3

Jack: (Looking up toward cloud) Shock! Horror! Terror! What are they? What's orange and tall and grows through clouds?

Jack's father: Giant Carrots! How dare fresh garden vegetables intrude into our polluted air! I'm going to see the giant about this.

Jack: Wait for me!

Child from Audience: Good riddance! Jack is climbing the giant carrot. (Jack and father climb carrots) Let's hope he stays in carrot Land.

Giants wife: (on cloud) Why are the carrot tops shaking?

Giant: It must be that pest Jack (Looks over the edge of cloud) He's climbing our carrots. That boy will never learn.

Magic hen: Bock, bock, bock, bock, bock! bock, bock, bock, bock, bock.

Giant's wife: Oh here's our magic hen. Can you help us?

hen: I'll drop a 24 carat gold egg on his head. (Lays eggs on Jack's head)

Jack: Help! Help!

Father: Heavenly eggs! (both drop dead)

This regular revue which the children write, perform in and compere is a wonderful forum for their using language to entertain.

Children learn language and its uses simultaneously. In fact, it is through its use that language is learned.

Frank Smith[6]

Forms of language

The second part of the scaffold is a classification of the real-world forms of printed text that the children may encounter in their lives.

Such a classification follows:

Advertisements
Agendas
Biographies
Captions
Cards (birthday, wedding, baby, sympathy, Mother's Day etc.)
Cartoons
Comics
Commercials
Diaries
Directions (how to make, how to use, how to play)
Fables
Factual text
Forms (to send for free samples, to enter competitions)
Graphs
Invitations
Interview forms
Jokes
Labelled diagrams
Letters
Letter-diaries
Limericks
Lists
Logs
Magazines
Maps
Menus
Myths
Newspapers (editorial, letters to editor, articles, sports and fashion, social column)
Notes
Plays
Poems
Posters
Programs
Radio scripts
Recipes
Reports (news, science)
Reviews (book, TV, film)
Riddles
Rhymes
Signs
Stories (adventure, detective, fairytale, fantasy, historical, sci-fi)
Summaries
Survey forms
Written conversations

If children are to be fully literate in our society, they will need to read and write in many different forms; in the process of learning about their worlds they will encounter many written forms. A well-rounded literacy program is one which ensures that they are exposed to a wide range of forms and which encourages their approximations of them.

A study of a language form: The Aboriginal myth

Leanne's Grade 3-4 children undertook an integrated learning unit on the early European settlement of Australia. The unit looked not only at European settlement but also at its effect on the traditional inhabitants, the Aborigines. Aboriginal myths tell much about the people: their affinity with the land, their belief in the Dreaming. It was therefore determined that one outcome of the unit would be the children's increased familiarity with and understanding of the Aboriginal myth.

During the first few weeks of the study dozens and dozens of myths were read aloud to the children and collections were left on the bookshelves for them to read. Once a week, after listening to several myths, the children worked in groups of four to list 'What we know about Aboriginal myths'.

After four such sessions, these were the statements of the various groups.

What we know about Aboriginal Myths

Aborigines told the myths.

Aboriginal myths have been passed down from aboriginal families.

We don't think the stories are true, but maybe some are.

Aborigines believe the Dreamtime stories.

They explain the past.

They tell us things from a long time ago.

They tell about how things became, e.g. Why the emu has no wings.

The stories are about nature, e.g. the sun, moon, stars, plants, animals, people.

They are not fairy tales.

Some Aboriginal myths are fairly short.

Aborigines sometimes told myths around the camp fire.

They tell aborigines about life before they were born.

At this point one group worked together with the teacher to write a myth, which was later published as beautiful big book, the title being *How the Koala Got His Black Button Nose*.

HOW THE KOALA GOT THE BLACK BUTTON NOSE.

A dreamtime story, written by Brook Dellamarta, Sally Edwards, Sallie Flynn, Taryn Gilpin, Gayle Patterson, Justin Wilkins.

A long, long time ago in the dreamtime, there lived a koala in a gum tree. He had a white nose and was round and chubby. He had small eyes and grey fur that covered his body.
When the sun was high in the sky the koala picked a gum leaf to eat but the leaf fell out of his paw, to the ground beneath. This leaf was the biggest and juiciest on the whole gum tree, so he raced down the tree before another koala could get the leaf.
Because the koala was running so fast he slipped over a big rock and fell head first into a puddle.
Poor koala. His fur was sticking together with black mud.
He headed straight for the waterfall to have a wash. When he stood under the waterfall he covered his nose because he did not want to get water up his nose.
He lay in the sun to dry. He did not know that there was mud on his nose. The sun baked the mud on his nose so hard he could not get the mud off.
That is why the koala has a black button nose.

Other children worked individually or in pairs to write myths. Here is the myth written by Brooke and Lauren.

How the kookaburra came to laugh.
One evening a kookaburra flew up a tree to go to bed. He was very sad. Because he was born sad and all the animals were sick and tired of seeing kookaburra being miserable so... That night all the animals except the kookaburra gathered around the fire to discuss what was to be done. The emu went forward and said, 'Come close, I've got a plan. Now I'll just go through our plan again. Kangaroo, you have to stand at the bottom. Wombat will stand on top of my head and then you will tickle kookaburra.' So all the animals hopped on top of one another. Suddenly they all fell over, the noise woke up kookaburra who started to laugh at such a funny sight. He laughed and laughed and has not stopped laughing ever since!

This study of Aboriginal myths was not a response to ticking off yet another written language form from a check list. Rather it was undertaken to assist the development of children's understanding of the culture of Australian Aborigines.

Relationship between forms and purposes

There is a relationship between language forms and language purposes: particular forms support and foster different uses. For example, letters, signs, posters and advertisements are language forms that can be used to direct and influence the behaviour of other people. Letters, diaries and poems can be vehicles for personal reflection. Riddles, songs, plays and personal anecdotes can entertain.

Audiences for language

The third part of the scaffold consists of the audiences for language. The three main broad audiences are:

- self
- known
- unknown

The particular audience a language user is addressing affects the demands placed upon that user. For example, when writing for oneself, it is not necessary to focus so much attention on sentence construction, spelling, punctuation or handwriting as when writing for someone else.

Even within the above three audience groups there are subcategories. For example, a known, trusted, friendly audience places different constraints on a language user from those of a known and hostile audience.

When planning a literacy program, a teacher needs (a) to be alert to the audiences his or her pupils are using language for, and (b) to ensure that children have experience in using language for different audiences.

Language is context–bound

Being knowledgeable about the purposes, forms and audiences for language is necessary if teachers are to plan well-rounded language programs. They should not use such knowledge as a series of check lists, ticking off each item as it is 'taught'. Rather such knowledge will help them to evaluate the breadth of their programs as well as to evaluate any given language event.

- 'What does this require of the child?'
- 'What is the purpose of the language?'
- 'For whom is the language intended?'
- 'In the real world, which written forms might be used to meet the intended purpose?'

Of course, the language event will be context-bound. For example, at the end of a unit on the environment the children may write to the local council suggesting improved recycling facilities in the area. The written form is a letter, the audience is unknown and the letter arises from the children's concern for their environment. The language is context-bound; it is authentic, not contrived.

If children are to use language for the widest range of purposes, forms and audiences (by being involved in authentic language events), they will engage in investigations in all curriculum areas. They will learn how to write a science report because they are engaging in scientific investigation, not just because the teacher wants them to learn how to write a science report.

To work scientifically involves predicting, experimenting, observing and concluding, as evidenced in the following report: 'Our Egg Experiment'. This particular experiment was just one of many which were all part of a study of 'Change' in Leanne's classroom.

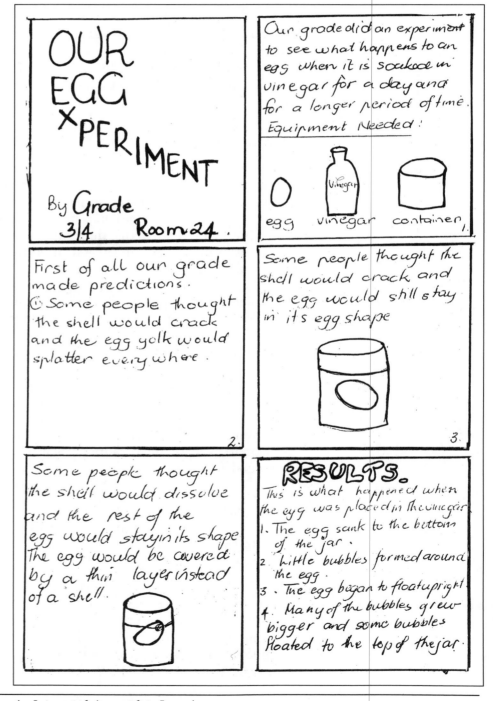

OUR EGG XPERIMENT
By Grade 3/4 Room 24.

Our grade did an experiment to see what happens to an egg when it is soaked in vinegar for a day and for a longer period of time. Equipment Needed:

egg   vinegar   container   1.

First of all our grade made predictions.
① Some people thought the shell would crack and the egg yolk would splatter every where.   2.

Some people thought the shell would crack and the egg would still stay in its egg shape   3.

Some people thought the shell would dissolve and the rest of the egg would stay in its shape The egg would be covered by a thin layer instead of a shell.

RESULTS.
This is what happened when the egg was placed in the vinegar
1. The egg sank to the bottom of the jar.
2. Little bubbles formed around the egg.
3. The egg began to float upright
4. Many of the bubbles grew bigger and some bubbles floated to the top of the jar.

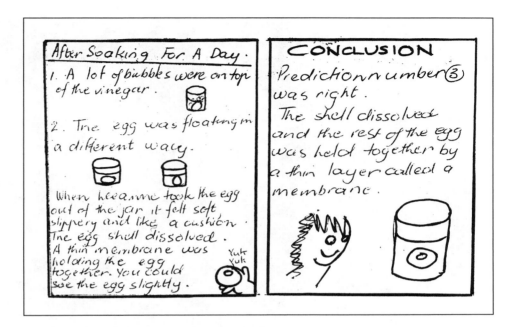

If children are experiencing language in a whole sense, they are encountering and using it for the widest possible range of purposes, forms and audiences. Of course, such language use occurs in context as children socialise, solve problems, reflect on personal experiences and take part in learning experiences set in all curriculum areas.

When planning for a continuing, cohesive, school-wide program, we ask:

- Which language purposes are we giving the children opportunities to use?
- Which language forms are we immersing our children in, modelling, and providing opportunity for them to try?
- Which audiences are the children using language for?

Remember, each language artifact is shaped by its own particular purpose, form and audience.

Students judge the best decorated fruit or vegetable at the Moonee Ponds West show

An Integrated Approach to Learning

Chapter 3 Shared contexts: School routines and special events

The classroom is an active social unit. The daily routines of the classroom and of the wider school community present a myriad of opportunities for developing language for authentic purposes, forms and audiences, all set in real-life context. Additionally, there are special class and school events which provide the context for learning many things together with language learning.

Routines

School assembly

A whole-school assembly is a regular Monday morning event, and for the past two years the conduct of the assembly has been the responsibility of the Grade 5-6 children. The children chosen to take the assembly do so for a whole semester; part of their weekly class work involves collecting information for the assembly from teachers, the principal, parent groups and the school diary, then drafting their script and rehearsing it.

Kate and Rebecca ran the assemblies during semester 4 of last year. For the final assembly before Christmas, Rebecca commenced at the microphone; Kate was nowhere to be seen. She was actually hiding behind a nearby building, dressed in a Father Christmas suit and waiting for a cue from Rebecca to make her entry. Here is just part of that Christmas script.

ASSEMBLY COMPARES SCRIPT

Hi, I'm Kate. We've got a lot of news for you. But....
    First the band will play

[music]

- Cross country on Wednesday. Good luck MPW
  On Friday MPW played Kensington for the scores...
  SPORTS REPORTS!
- Would Mr. Smith like to say anything?
  Would Miss. Fleming like to say anything?
- Just a reminder, no school on Tuesday.
  And book bazzare 24-28. All children + parents welcome from 8-7 to browse + buy.
- And Claire & Michelle from PFCT have some news
  This morning there will be a coffee morning held by the P.F.A in room 9. All parents who are here this morning are welcome. Please come!
- Pick up your bags and go in.

Christmas script

                              Written by Kate Shadbolt

Hey guess what kids I asked Santa to come and see us for our last assembally and he said that he may come and see us (ringing of bells). Slow down dasher, dancer, prancer, vicson, commet, cupid, donner and bitzen. Ho, Ho, Ho. Merry Christmas everybody. What would you like for Christmas Rebecca. Ah ... a bike, roller skates ... Oh I nearly forgot a puppy.

And what would you like little boy (they tell me what they want). (Ask about 6 people). Shirl I bet you want chocolate! OK Rebecca whats next ... the reminders of the week Santa. Ho.

1. I'm going to get my suit mended.
2. Feed the raindeer.

NO ... NOT YOUR reminders of the week MPW'S.

Break up at 1.30 p.m.

Anyway I've got to go and have my photos taken with the kids at Highpoint.

Sports reports

Following interschool sport, participating children are chosen to draft reports and then read them at the Monday assembly. The children are encouraged to be creative — to avoid statements such as:

'On Friday we played netball against Ascot Vale. The scores were MPW 16, Ascot Vale 9.'

This is not acceptable.

footy

there we were it was our first footy match. there was a capacity crowd 3 men, a dog and 2 seagulls. D.M lit us up and we sizzled away leaveing A.V in the Ashes. the scores were A.V 8 to M.P.W 18. M.P.W was so hot the fire engine had to put us Out after the game. we would like to thank the umpirs for providing us with the matches!!

And here we are at Wimbletor...no, thats wrong... Its... M P W and M P W are playing Ascot Vale. We're sitting by the bat tennis court and watching three games at the same time. The final scors are

MPW 45
to

A. Vale 36

When much time was being devoted to poetry in the Grade 5-6 room, one report was presented as a poem.

Office duty

Grade 5-6 children are rostered to attend the office and answer the telephone at lunch time. Through answering the phone, making announcements over the loudspeaker and seeking out teachers, the children's oral language skills have improved greatly. Many callers have complimented the school on the way the children have handled their requests.

Collection of money

The chore of collecting various moneys (for sports, camp, special lunch, excursions) is often given to the children, along with the responsibility of counting and checking the total amount. This is maths being used for authentic purpose.

Class diary

At the end of the day, each grade gathers on the floor and reflects upon the day's happenings. Comments are written as diary entries onto a large sheet of paper that hangs on the wall: initially the teacher scribed, but now the children are eager to volunteer their services. After two or three weeks the entries are typed up and illustrated; at the end of semester, all the entries are collated and published as a class diary.

THURSDAY 16th Feb:

"I wobble when I do it!" says Aaron.
What does he do???????
You wouldn't believe it...........
We voted to have homework!!!!!!!!!

THURSDAY 2nd March:

Today is HOT.....It's as hot as.....
Sizzling sausages, sizzling in the sun.
An oven.
A turkey in the oven ready to be served for a Christmas dinner.
Boiling fat in a frypan.
An overheated engine in the car.

WEDNESDAY 5th April:

Library begins for term 2 with 45 minutes of myths and legends.
Here comes Angry Anderson?.....No.
A Hari Krishna?.....No.
Humpty Dumpty's cousin?.......No.
IT'S FRANK SMITH.

Games

Among the expectations in Grade 5-6 is that the children will learn to play some of the old-fashioned strategy games such as chess, draughts, Chinese chequers and backgammon, as well as some of the newer ones — for instance, Othello, Cluedo and UNO (these not so much for strategy as for practice in adding up scores and keeping running totals).

Children are involved in teaching one another to play, and the names of those who have mastered particular games are recorded on a chart. Once enough children know how to play, class championships are organised — by the children. They draw up the fixtures and record the results.

Evaluation

Evaluation is a regular aspect of the child's classroom activities. Children are regularly asked to evaluate and comment upon:

- themselves (effort, understanding, attitudes, abilities etc.);
- the programs (literature, maths, FAT etc.);
- special activities (camp, billycart grand prix, excursions etc.).

Impressed upon the children is the need for thoughtfulness and honesty, since their teachers are genuinely interested in what they have to say. They are told that their personal assessments will help to determine the teachers' expectations for them — that their own evaluation of their strengths, weaknesses and areas needing improvement will be considered by the teachers when planning programs for them. At the start of the year, this evaluation takes the following form.

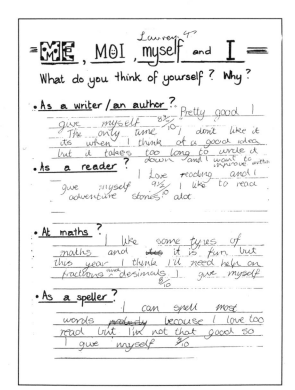
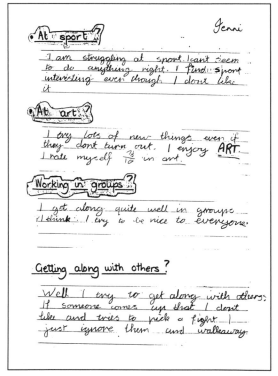

As the year progresses the children are asked to comment on specific aspects of their learning, behaviour and attitudes.

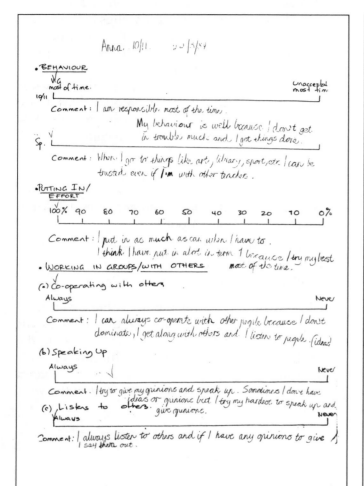

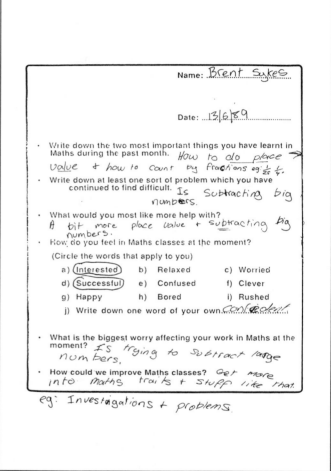

At mid-year, the children's 'self-report' is used as a basis for parent–teacher interviews (which the children attend). They are asked to be completely honest with themselves; the self-report is conferenced by the teacher and if there is a difference of opinion between child's and teacher's evaluation, the question may be asked, 'Do you really believe you are like that?' However, no child is forced to amend his or her report. Areas in which the child's view differs from the teacher's view form an interesting basis for discussion.

CIRCLE EITHER 1, 2 or 3 BELOW DEPENDING ON WHICH
DESCRIPTION YOU THINK MOST APPLIES TO YOU.

1 = It's a struggle. I'm not confident and
    find things usually very difficult.

2 = Average. I usually cope OK with most things.

3 = No problem! Very confident! My performance,
    ideas, etc. are usually excellent.

THEN WRITE A COMMENT.

AREA	ASSESSMENT			COMMENTS
READING .... (literature and silent reading)	1	2	③	I like reading alot and I'm pretty good at literature.
WRITING .... (personal writing, year book, personal journal)	1	2	③	My writing is very neat and my stories and comments are very good.
WEEKLY WONDERS ...	1	②	3	I find weekly wonders average Sometimes its hard to get humorous answers.
WORD STUDY	1	2	③	I am very good at spelling, I find wordstudy pretty easy.
THEMEWORK	1	②	3	I find themework average. It can get hard.
LIBRARY	1	2	③	I like going to the library. No problems.
P.E.	1	②	3	I'm not very good at sport. I don't like it much, either.
ART	1	②	3	I like art. I don't find it that difficult.

GENERAL BEHAVIOUR, ATTITUDE, and WORK HABITS.

Tick the appropriate box for you.	Not at all	A little bit	A fair bit	A lot
1. Can work without constant supervision.				✓
2. Can hear others (including friends) without being talkative or disruptive.		✓		
3. Is considerate of other's feelings and / or ideas.			✓	
4. Can work well as part of a small or large group.			✓	
5. Tries to do well at all tasks – at all times.				✓
6. Worries about work.		✓		
7. Accepts responsibility.				✓
8. Is confident and prepared to have a guess / take a risk.			✓	
9. Co-operates well with others.			✓	
10. Likes working alone.				✓
11. Is interested and involved in class activities.			✓	
12. Is confident about tackling new tasks			✓	
13. Enjoys discussions and confidently shares own ideas and opinions.			✓	

"General Comment"

Being in the CC5 is sometimes nerve-racking, because I am the only grade 5 in there, and the Grade 6s make me feel like a baby!

I'm usually relaxed in here, my feelings since term 1 have changed; I was scared stiff then! Usually I am fine, with no worries, coping O.K, but sometimes I can have these "fits" when I feel let down, and my work goes down.

MATHS EVALUATION

① CIRCLE THE DESCRIPTION YOU THINK BEST DESCRIBES YOU WITH REGARD TO MATHS.

(a) I struggle. Find maths puzzling and difficult.   (b) ⟨I can cope well with most of it. I am average.⟩   (c) No problems. Very good at maths.

② PLACE A TICK IN THE APPROPRIATE BOX TO INDICATE YOUR ANSWER.

	Not at all	A little bit	A fair bit	A lot
(a) How much do you look forward to maths.		✓		
(b) How often do you feel bored.		✓		
(c) How often do you ask questions when you don't understand things.		✓		
(d) How often do you feel you don't understand.			✓	

③ I LIKE maths when we have activity maths and corect homework and when we go out-side and do mesurements and maths games

④ I DON'T LIKE maths when we do stuff on decimals and factions

The children even evaluate the parent–teacher–child interview.

Children are constantly asked to evaluate the classroom program and special happenings within the school. Their comments and suggestions are valued and are used to help plan future activities and change aspects of the program.

Kids, Parent Teacher interview.

2.00 pm — biting nails down to the quick! worried sick about parent teacher interviews.

2.40 pm — go into parent-teacher interview..... When I was reading out my Evaluation it struck — THE NERVOUS TWITCH! I tried to stop my leg going up and down — it didn't work but then it suddenly stopped. I then read out the rest — it went well "phew"

3.00 pm — "phew" — its all over. It wasn't hard at all now I'm free......

Plan of attack

I plan to try and ignore people when they hit me and to not react when people tease me on call me names. I am going to work on my group skills and try to fit in with people.

General Program Evaluation

What I enjoyed this term?
Literature — I enjoyed reading Tom's Midnight Garden, maths Because we have a lot more activites.

What I would like to see continued?
More work on place value in maths.

What I didn't enjoy this term.
Having to do Beat the tape once a week. I passed tape 18.

What I would like to see changed......
Literature — let the Kids Read Books that they chose, this MAY improve Reading.

The nicest thing that happened to me this term
Having 3 nights sleep on school camp.

What disappointed me most was
Nothing that I can think of at the moment.

What I most need to work on is......
Getting my work into my Book and asking for help, trying to understand and Be like others.

On Thursday night I was wishing it was Friday as Friday was going to be the perfect day at school because it was a F.A.T. day.
Before Friday we had to make up a timetable so we could organize what we were going to do.
Friday turned out to be just like I thought it would turn out. I'd love to have another F.A.T. day.

Rebecca.

Show Day

I thought Show Day was great. There were heaps of different side shows, some of them were shooting ducks, He-Men throwing balls through holes. I think the best one was the wet sponge competition. You had to throw a wet sponge at a persons face. They didn't cost anything except for George's but that one had really good prizes. All of them had prizes but that one had the best.

Dean Linardos

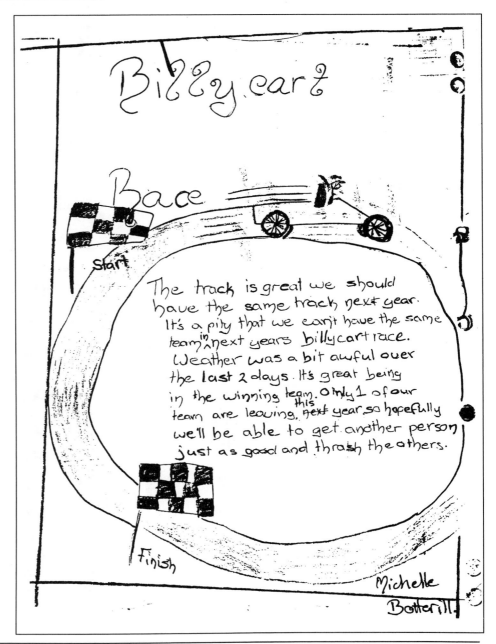

Billy cart Race

Start

Finish

The track is great we should have the same track next year. It's a pity that we can't have the same team in next years billy cart race. Weather was a bit awful over the last 2 days. It's great being in the winning team. Only 1 of our team are leaving this year, so hopefully we'll be able to get another person just as good and thrash the others.

Michelle Botterill

Children's timetable plans

To help children work towards becoming self-disciplined, organised and motivated learners, Shirl and David have recently instituted a process by which a number of them are encouraged to plan a week's work for themselves. They must draw up a detailed timetable for their week, have it conferenced and approved, carry it out and then evaluate it. The whole operation is a real-life exercise in planning, operating and evaluating.

Plan Your Own Time Table

It wasn't easy to stick to my time table because if the rest of the grade did something that you had to do you missed out, or you didn't go by your time table. And it was easy to behave responsibly. Most of the time I was able to stay in a "working mood". I over planned and under planned and once I was exact I would do it again but if something had to be done, or special work that every body had to do I would make sure it was on everybodys time table, overall I rate it 9/10.

Lauren T

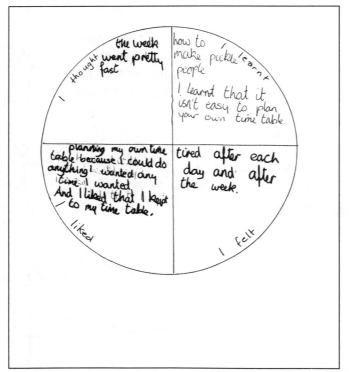

Special events

There are many other events — generally one-off yearly events — that are part of the class calendar and that provide opportunities for the children to engage in a broad range of cross-curricula learning activities. They are given responsibility for much of the planning, organisation, running and evaluation of the activities and events.

Easter Hat Parade

Every year Moonee Ponds West has an Easter Hat Parade. This year one of the teachers suggested that the parade be followed by some Easter games, to involve as many grades as were interested. The whole school decided it would be fun. The Grade 5-6 class committee offered to plan enough activities to cater for 240 children; they took on a major organising role and decided on twenty suitable activities, working out what was involved in each activity and where each was to be run, collecting the equipment, organising leaders for each activity (since there weren't enough staff, this involved writing to parents to ask for help) and so on.

To the children's credit, the day was great fun. Most of them wanted to continue until home time. Those responsible for the organising commented on how exhausting and time-consuming the task was and how they could appreciate what teachers ordinarily had to go through.

Show Day

An even more demanding task taken on by the children was that of organising the annual MPW Show for the Grade 3-6 children. The teachers assumed a co-ordinating role, but the bulk of the details were worked out by the children. The Show lasted the whole morning and involved a number of competitions such as:

Best decorated fruit/vegie
Best country picture
Longest torn Mintie wrapper
Best decorated biscuit
Most human-looking spud
Best paper weaving

There were also outdoor events, such as rope climbing. Judges had to be chosen, judging criteria established, rosettes and sashes made and presented.

The children worked feverishly for several weeks creating their own sideshows. These proved to be as popular as those of the real Show.

The morning culminated in a Grand Parade, with children in small groups taking roles as pets or masters and putting on performances in front of the judges (two teachers, two parents, two children).

Throughout this event the children were engaged in many different thought processes: predicting, questioning, planning, analysing, problem solving, evaluating, comparing. Activities came from many curriculum areas — art, maths, social studies and language.

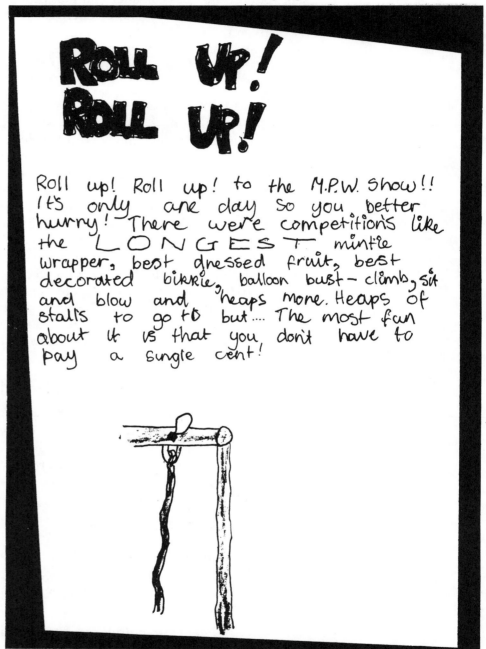

ROLL UP! ROLL UP!

Roll up! Roll up! to the M.P.W. show!! It's only one day so you better hurry! There were competition's like the LONGEST mintie wrapper, best dressed fruit, best decorated bikkie, balloon bust — climb, sit and blow and heaps more. Heaps of stalls to go to but..... The most fun about it is that you don't have to pay a single cent!

End-of-year break-up

For the past four years the Grade 5–6 children have chosen to have their end-of-year break-up in the form of a formal, sit-down lunch. This means having a long table with table decorations and place-names, and best dress for the children.

The menu consists of:

> Nibbles
> Roast chicken, roast potatoes, peas, green salad
> Plum pudding, cream or ice-cream, custard

This is followed by a dance, with a video for those who are not interested in dancing.

The children are given the task of costing and ordering the luncheon. They work out what and how much food is needed, phone relevant take-away food outlets, obtain quotes, work out the cost per head and finally arrange for delivery. Much real-world maths at work.

School camp

A fine example of integrated learning is that of the school-camp booklet. It has always been a major chore for the teachers to organise this booklet, writing out lists of children attending, room groups, duty groups and so on. Timetables have to be drawn up, rules formulated, and diary pages drawn up.

Now, however, the children organise this publication. The class committee has the responsibility of finding a group of children to co-ordinate the job. Teachers are allocated certain pages to complete (for example, the activities timetable and the camp quiz), and various children volunteer to supply other pages.

This writing activity has real purpose. The success of the camp is largely dependent on the booklet, for all the camp organisation is contained therein. Much of the language used is to direct or regulate, some of it is to entertain, and the audience is, of course, a known one — classmates attending the camp. Because the writing activity is authentic, the children are alert to the need for accuracy of information and attention to handwriting and spelling, as well as to layout.

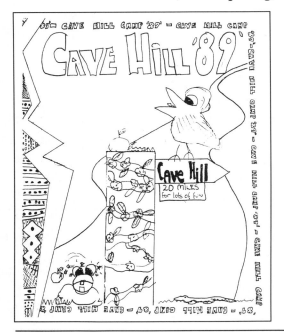

Children as organisers

Franca, a Grade 6 girl, has this to say about children assuming responsibility for the organisation of school events. (It's not absolutely true that 'the teachers don't do a thing'! They do help to get some children started, sit in on rehearsals and so on.)

Children Organising Activities

Franca

In 10/11 D.M. and Shirl (our teachers) plan to do activities but choose a group of kids to organise it and to explain to everybody about it ⁻ᵉʷsometimes they even run it!   A group of kids have been chosen to organise the M.P.W. Billy Cart Grand Prix, that means they organise the course, arrange the heats evenly according to the kids in the team, they write letters to parents so they can see what the M.P.W. Grand Prix is all about, they make signs, make medals, cups and sashes.   They also make up entry forms for teams to fill out, which includes the kids' names, what the billy-cart is called and what grade they are in.

Another time where kids have been chosen to organise is our Termly Revue.   Two children are chosen to compere our Revue. Groups of kids get together and make up some sort of play, dance, rhymes, shadow puppet plays, etc.   The comperes see the act to see whether or not the act is good enough to be put on for our Revue.   The comperes also make a list of items, put them in order, introduce our Revue to the audience and sometimes introduce the plays.   Kids that are chosen to organise things are very responsible.   They have to co-operate with other people.
But would you believe it the teachers don't do a thing!
The work is left to the kids to organise.   If a group has trouble they go around asking people what they think should happen.
They take ideas from kids and if they are good they use them for some sort of activity.

Chapter 4 Shared contexts: The integrated learning unit

The basic assumption underlying the integrative approach is that knowledge is not rigidly compartmentalised, but that given any object, process, person, event etc. one may focus attention on its social implications, its scientific aspects, its economic connotations, its historical context, its aesthetic component, its personal significance and so on.

The Primary School Curriculum: A Manual for Schools[7]

Children do not naturally think and view learning in terms of isolated subject areas, but rather have a holistic outlook on life. This outlook should be reflected in the way the teacher teaches, the way planning is done, the way the timetable is structured.

To prevent learning from being fragmented and therefore not as relevant to the children's lives as it might be, we plan integrated units based on an inquiry approach to learning, in which the children are not passive

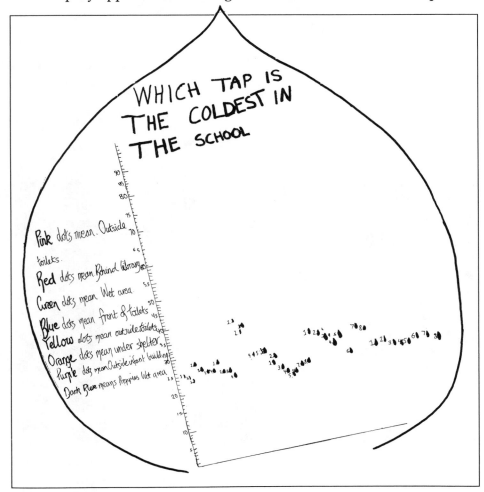

Children read quietly, seated on comfortable lounge chairs. Behind them is a display of individual children's maths investigations

but active participants who are encouraged to think critically and to question the world they live in.

Rather than the class program being a collection of unrelated activities from different curriculum areas, we focus upon what the children already know, the things they want to know, and how together we can find answers. The children have important input into the development and direction of the units. Their initial statements of understanding, and their questions, provide the basis for our planning and are constantly referred to and refined throughout the unit.

Selection of activities

When planning, we incorporate all sections of the curriculum where possible. We attempt to integrate all areas of learning, but it is sometimes difficult or impractical to do so; activities from any one curriculum area are included only when they genuinely help to bring children to the understandings set out at the start of the unit. For example, maths activities are included not for the sake of doing maths but because they will contribute to the children's understanding of the topic. As part of a unit on water, for instance, a picture graph was compiled to indicate which drinking tap provided the coolest water on a hot day.

By continually relating the activities to the focus questions and statements of understandings, the learning is more relevant and meaningful to the children. Planning for an integrated curriculum takes time, effort and practice — planning with groups of teachers is easier than doing it alone. However, although the initial planning is time-consuming, it is worth the effort: the class program is less fragmented and tedious and more cohesive and interesting, and the children are alert — thinking, questioning and working together co-operatively.

Selection of topics or units

The selection of the topic or integrated unit is of great importance. What makes for a successful unit? Of course, the success of a unit can only be gauged against the expressed hoped-for outcomes, but in general terms would take account of both the children's level of involvement throughout the unit and the growth of their understanding of the topic.

In selection, it might prove helpful to consider the following questions.

- Does the topic have potential for the development of concepts which form the basis of the social and physical study of the world? Examples of such concepts are social organisation, culture, energy and matter.
- Does the topic have potential for the children to hook onto or to engage with and extend their own present understandings of the world?
- Does the topic have the potential for learning to occur in ways which are compatible with the children's stages of cognitive development and their present interest levels?
- Are there sufficient resources (human and other) available to allow for an inquiry-based approach to the topic?

Set out below is a model for planning integrated units of work, devised by Julie Hamston; it is based on key elements in *The Social Education Framework* P–10.[8] David, Shirl and Leanne use this model as a guide when planning their units.

- Focus questions
- Contributing questions

Knowledge	Skills	Values	Action
Understandings Concepts Facts	*e.g.:* Critical thinking Social interaction Communication Research	*e.g.:* Equality Co-operation Respect for others Tolerance	Applying learning to some sort of social action

Inquiry	Related activities
Acquaintance activity Gathering information Organising information Drawing together (The inquiry process is not inflexible; for example, after reaching the organising stage, there may be a need to gather more information.)	These are activities which relate to the topic being investigated, but are not necessarily part of the inquiry process. They need not be undertaken by all children.

Inquiry model [9]

Acquaintance activity/Confrontation activity
    Example: Something to interest or motivate the children, such as an excursion, a video, an experiment or a brainstorming activity to tap children's knowledge.

Gathering information
    Example: Collecting resources, researching, interviewing.

Organising information
    Example: Making charts, graphs; presenting findings.

Drawing together
    Example: Expressing understandings, making generalisations.

For practical illustrations of integrated learning units, see Appendix 1.

Chapter 5 Personal contexts

An integrated curriculum provides opportunities for the children to bring into the classroom their individual worlds, their individual interests. Occasionally these relate to the integrated unit of study; more often they don't. Time is provided throughout the school week for children to pursue these interests; this contributes to their being able to take some control and responsibility over their learning.

Personal writing

Two or three sessions a week may be devoted to personal writing. This is where children have full control over their writing in that they determine the form, purpose and audience. They may write in their diaries, or they may write letters, poems, stories, 'How to' manuals, factual texts or captions for photos. The writing may relate to the unit of work, or it may not. Some examples are reproduced here.

Amanda, Grade 3, wrote a poem about school for the school magazine — quite a wide audience.

Amanda

At school.....
We do lots of things.
Some times we play games.
Activities I enjoy.

At school........
Maths session is so much fun
I feel sad when they're all done.
Play time is that sun out?.
I asks if I can play with people.

At school.......
writing in folder to be finished
I am publishing a book
everyone takes a look

At school.........
School is over to a end
and then we will start All over again

A Grade 6 pupil reads a book published by one of her classmates

An Integrated Approach to Learning

Mark, a very mature Grade 6 boy with an interesting sense of humour, has a wide range of interests. He has developed a love of reading only over the past fifteen months, and now Tolkien is his favourite author. When Mark first arrived at the school he found it very difficult to write or produce anything in language sessions, even though the choice of topic and style of writing was his. After much discussion and negotiation with his teachers, it was discovered that he had an interest in wasps. Mark listed first all the facts he knew about wasps and then the questions to which he wanted answers. He then happily researched the answers. He is now publishing this piece — something that is of genuine interest to him. Some extracts from his piece on wasps are included.

Imagine it ...... you're sitting there at a picnic, not a cloud in the sky ...... just a whasp!
A WASP!!!
If its not flies or ants — its wasps.
I hate wasps.
Let me tell you about wasps.
• There are more than 17 000 species of wasps (and that's a lot of wasps!)
• About 3800 kinds of wasps are found in America and Canada (and they can have them!!)
• Wasps nests are different because of the materials used to build them (but not bricks!)
• The wasps body like other insects is made up of three parts and has six legs.
• Oh, and if you see a wasp don't try and kill it, because you may end up will all his pals after you. (But there isn't any wasps phone box around.
How do they do it.)

Joanne is an avid reader. She particularly loves to read the poetry of Robin Klein, Alan Ahlberg and Brian Patten. She loves to write poems. She whips them up at lunchtime, at home and (of course) in school. Often Joanne's response to a classroom experience is a poem.

```
            CAMP

Ready
On bus
Going to sleep
Arriving at Sovereign Hill
School

School
Getting changed
On Mine tour
Buying things in town
Camp

Camp
Getting unpacked
Having delicious dinner
Going Bowling in town
Bed

Bed
Getting dressed
Packing my clothes
Having cornflakes for breakfast
Full

Full
Bags away
All cabins locked
Getting old  ?  again
School

School
Supplied lunch
Back to school
Having free time again
Camp

Camp
Getting bags
Getting on bus
Starting to go home
Home

I think Sovereign Hill was grouse with

a capital G.  It was really

interesting.
```

```
IT WAS ...

Big
Huge
Roomy

IT WAS ...

A very cold school
Very dark
Being awed at the sight of it

IT WAS ...

Being divided into groups
Walking around the school
Looking in all the classrooms.

IT WAS ...

Swapping over groups
Slaving away on the bike
in the fitness course

IT WAS ...

Good
But  BORING
```

```
                    ESSENDON HIGH

We got on the bus
3 to a seat
At least there wasn't
Very much heat.

When we got there
We got out of the bus
Were divided into groups
And made a very big fuss.

We went off in our groups
And were shown all around
We met some old friends
Who shouted while we frowned.

Then we swapped our groups
And we went to a gym
They had a course there
To keep us slim.

Then we went back
To the bus
Where there was
a very big fuss.

They had more fun
Than us
We were grumbling
As we got on the bus.

It was alright up at Essendon High
But it was boring in the end
And on the bus good luck left me
I didn't get to sit with a friend!!!
```

Presently Joanne is publishing a selection of her poems — poems which cover a wide range of subjects.

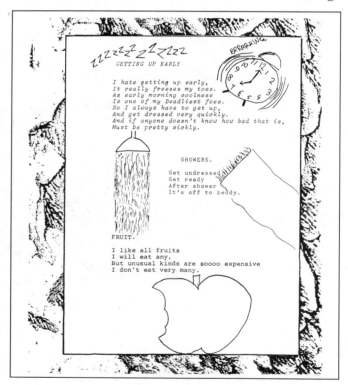

Joanne's very particular interest in poetry is encouraged by her teachers. The class programming is such that she has much opportunity in school time to follow this personal interest.

Share time: Interests and hobbies

Children in Shirl and David's 5-6 have opportunities to share their hobbies with the rest of the grade. The teachers do little to organise these sessions. The presenters determine how they will use their 10 minutes, what materials they will need and how the audience is to be seated. Many of the children script what they are going to say, others just jot down reminders, while some use language sessions to rehearse.

- Bruno, Grade 6, shared his interest in marbles — he brought along his personal collection; he talked about the differences between them, his favourite ones, how he became interested and the games he plays. He then selected some children unfamiliar with marbles to play around with them.
- Rebecca, Grade 6, came dressed in Spanish costume and proceeded to give a display of Spanish dancing accompanied by music. Later she explained some of the history of the dancing, demonstrated some of the simpler steps and chatted about her costume.
- Max, Grade 6, armed with his collection of matchbox cars, told his eager audience about his favourite cars: the games he and his brother play with them, where he got them from and the relative cost of each one.

The audience (the rest of the children) are encouraged to ask questions throughout the sharing and at its conclusion to comment constructively on the session: for instance, how it went, and how it might have been improved!

Many of these individual sharings provide the impetus for the children to write or publish a book on their interests. For the children sharing, the planning, organising, reading, writing and speaking have a real purpose.

The hall program

This program, in which children from various home groups take part, provides many opportunities for them to pursue individual interests. A writing area is set up in the hall. Many children write and address letters to friends and teachers in classrooms throughout the school. The letters are posted in a mailbox, which is later cleared, and are delivered to individual letter boxes outside the classrooms.

Lin, a Grade 2 girl, made use of some discarded wedding cards to write to her teacher, Leanne, a few days before her wedding.

Take-home book program

The take-home book program enables children throughout the school to pursue individual reading interests. Each day they may select books of their choice from a wide range of literature. For quite a long while David, a Grade 3 boy, borrowed 'Meg and Mog' books, and this interest carried over to his writing. One piece David wrote during personal writing was 'Meg's Flying Car'.

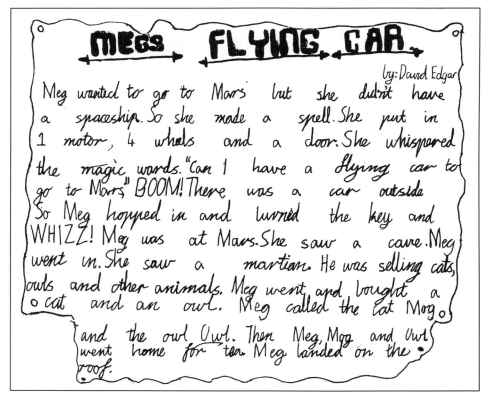

Grade 5–6 literature program

Over the past four or five years the literature program in Grade 5–6 consisted of groups of six to eight children reading the same book at the same time at the same rate — perhaps a chapter or two a week — with some choice in the selection of their books. Many of the more able readers expressed dissatisfaction with this organisation. They felt restricted in the number and range of books they were reading.

The literature program has since been changed. It now allows individual children to:

- select books they want to read;
- read them at their own rates;
- choose reading partners, if desired;
- choose whether they wish to respond, and if so, how;
- share with teachers and other children their reactions to the books, experiences they may have in common with the characters, and parts they have particularly enjoyed.

The children's evaluations are highly favourable to the new organisation.

> I think its much more Fun that last year (keep it that way.... please)

> Literiture- because I had a more range of books to read, and I could read at my own pace. (Kate·B.)

Michael responded to *Midnite*, by Randolph Stow, by creating a life-size model of the bushranger Midnite. The model now sits quietly in the classroom and is often mistaken for one of the children.

Having finished reading *Hating Alison Ashley*, Max drafted a letter to Robin Klein expressing his thoughts and views on the book.

> Dear Robin Klein
> I thought your book got off to a slow start but I just knew it was going to get exciting! You definitely put in suspense. I wouldn't of liked to be Erica on drama night though I have been in her position before but it wasn't that bad! I didn't think Erk and Alison would make friends. The Basin skins sounded like a pretty bad gang. After they wrote on the window with mud on the camp. It wasn't a bad literature book. I gave it a rating of 7/10!

Kate, after reading *The Present Takers*, kept a diary as Lucy Hall, the main character in the book.

Dear Diary.

am Today it was my birthday. Dad brought the new shoes. I am wearing them to school.

pm. Melanie Prosser and her gang "bullyed me. They made me bring presents for them tomorrow. Angus wants me to meet him at the cross-roads. YUK!

Melanie looks like this

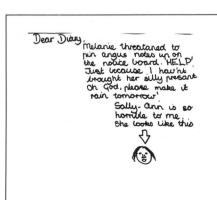

Dear Diary. Melanie threatened to pin angus notes up on the notice board. HELP! Just because I havn't brought her silly present Oh God, please make it rain tomorrow!
Sally-Ann is so horrible to me. She looks like this

Dear Diary It did not rain.

Dear Diary
am The weekend was so peaceful without melanie bothering me. Heck God, she's here now! Help!

pm. melanie made me shoplift today. Because of her dumb present. we got in BIG trouble.

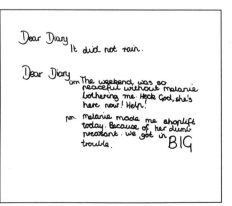

Personal journals

Each year, Samantha spent an extended holiday with her family in Queensland. Of her own volition, she wrote in her diary for the entire period that she was away — in Adrian Mole style.

Holiday Diary, Samantha.

Day 1. Left home at 3.45 a.m. this morning. Drove for 14 hours. Stayed at Motel called 'The Burk and Wills Motel' in Moree. Got sick — listened to music.

Day 2. Drove for another 6 hrs. Arrived in Brisbane at 2.30 at my Auntie's. Ran over a bird. Sizzled like silly 'cos it was so hot. Went to Brisbane Bot. Gardens. Bought 4 garfield stickers and a Garfield Book mark. Listened to music.

Day 3. Went to disco called Sibyls withs my cousins. Won 2 free tickets in dancing comp. The D.J. called me Maddonna . . . The was a real NERD there and he danced real YUKKK. I'll show you how when I get back to Melbourne.

Day 4. Hired a bike and went for a ride. Went to a real old house for a sticky beak.

Day 6. Went to doctor's (female) only to find I have Bronchitis and an infected ear. Went to an old friend's and had same dinner as last year (chicken and garlic).

Day 19. Bought Countdown Mag. Maybe found a pen friend (a boy, but I don't care. I have the same interests as him). Went to library. Borrowed Penny Pollard's letters. (It's grouse).

Other children use their personal journals or letter-diaries as sounding boards for problems they're having at home or at school. They may seek clarification about or advice on particular matters; sometimes they just want someone to listen or to share something with. The children who lack the confidence to approach their teachers directly can feel quite safe and secure in using their personal journals.

To Shirl.
iearn Having a lote of Travabl with
worke at Scool Because my Braver
teases me i Hate my Braver
He Perobaly Hate me to i Gese your
Perobaly wondering wy i Havent
Ben Doing my worke Reply its Because
of things at Home Got to go
Bye

Journal entries can also provide uninvited feedback on the classroom and program.

Personal maths investigations

Lisa was looking for a new area to explore in personal maths. When talking with her teacher, she mentioned having pen friends in Canada and the United States of America, and commented upon the cost of sending letters overseas. This discussion lead to Lisa's undertaking a whole range of maths-based activities, all related to pen friends; for example:

- how long it takes for a letter to reach Manitoba (Canada) and Salt Lake City (USA) via both air and surface mail;
- the cost of aerograms compared with that of the letters she was sending;
- the time differences between these two cities and Melbourne;
- the costs of phone calls in peak periods and off-peak periods compared with costs of letters.

For her personal maths investigation, Olga (8 years) decided to find out how many hours she was at school each week.

How many hours we stay at school?

L. Nelson
24·10·89

Plan.

(1) Find out how many hours we stay at school for one day.

(2) Then find out how many hours in 5 day's ~~in school~~ at school

① Hours we stay in 1 day.

6 and a half hours.

5 Days = 32 and a half hours.

How to present:

Rule up a chart with the five school days then write the hours we stay for then write the answer at the bottom.

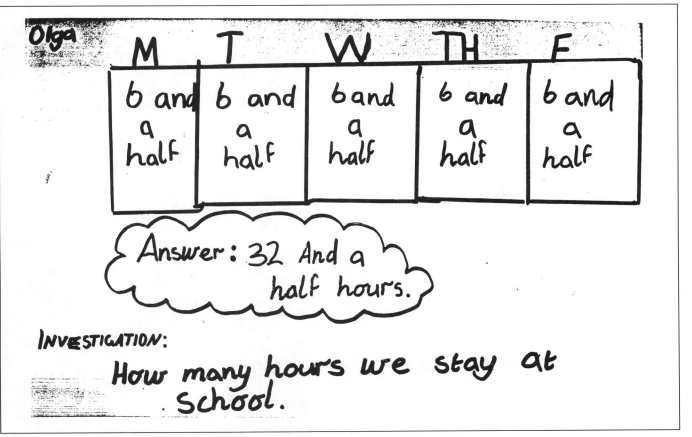

Olga

M	T	W	TH	F
6 and a half	6 and a half	6 and a half	6 and a half	6 and a half

Answer: 32 And a half hours.

INVESTIGATION:
How many hours we stay at school.

Brendan, 7 years, decided he would investigate how many push-ups he could do in three minutes. He retired with a friend to a corner of the room where there was enough space to do the push-ups. The friend had to watch the 3-minute timer and count the push-ups: in 33° heat, Brendan managed eighty-eight push-ups in 3 minutes.

In personal maths, as in personal writing, the children take control of their learning. They identify investigations which have relevance to their lives and which are of interest to them. They then plan how they will carry out the investigations, listing any necessary materials. This plan is conferenced with the teacher before the child proceeds with the investigation.

Children working in twos or threes in Leanne's Grade 2–3 classroom

An Integrated Approach to Learning

Chapter 6 The integrated curriculum: Skill development

Where language is integrated with learning across the curriculum, how are the skills taught? When this is asked, the questioner generally is referring to what were traditionally known as the skills: spelling, handwriting, grammar and punctuation — the things once taught in careful sequence as small, separate pieces from grade-labelled packages. For example, first we only allowed children to practise writing straight letters, such as 'i' and 'l'. Next we introduced them to round letters such as 'o' and 'c', and then were they permitted to practise letters that are both round and straight, such as 'd'. Today we know better. We've all seen four-, five- and six-year-olds write their names and also write for a range of purposes, and the letters they select are those they need to make their messages, not the easy, straight letters or the supposedly more difficult round ones.

Skills such as spelling and handwriting are learned whenever the children are using language, be it in listening to a factual text about whales, writing a report after a science experiment or sharing a big book of rhymes with a group. The nature of language is such that when it is being used for a real-life purpose, all the subsystems are present and are being used in an interwoven way. This is whole language.[10] Cambourne refers to Nancy Atwell's 'coaxial cable' metaphor of whole language.

The 'coaxial cable' metaphor

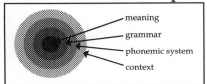

- meaning
- grammar
- phonemic system
- context

This metaphor views language as a network of interlocking systems, all of which operate simultaneously. Language has an inner core of meaning which is wrapped in outer layers of phonemic, grammatical, pragmatic systems.

Brian Cambourne [11]

Writing a science report is a demonstration of the genre of a science report as well as a demonstration of grammar, of spelling, of lettering and of punctuation. Writing a letter of thanks requires the writer to draw upon knowledge of letter writing as well as of spelling, punctuation, grammar, letter formation, and how to put all these together to convey the intended meaning.

When working with whole text, the learner may at any time focus on any one of the subsystems. When reading a book in a shared-reading situation, the children's attention may be drawn to the use of large lettering for words of emphasis, or perhaps to the use of direct speech. On yet another occasion the focus may be upon some interesting spelling patterns. Of course, in a single language demonstration different children may focus on different language features.

So, for example, children who are taking part in Readers' Theatre (where they read the parts of the characters in a story and a narrator reads the text that is not in direct speech) may well clarify their understandings about direct speech and the use of talking marks in written text:

And Hattie said,
'Goodness gracious me!
I can see a nose, two eyes
and two ears in the bushes!'[12]

All the subsystems of language are present in this demonstration of text. As it is read aloud, the child who is Hattie must know when the character actually begins speaking. The talking marks are one indicator. (See Appendix 2 for procedure in Readers' Theatre.)

In a Grade 1–2–3 classroom, after several readings of *Mr Gumpy's Outing* the children and teacher together compiled a list of all the 'ed' words from one particular page — the page describing how the animals all misbehaved.[13]

The children could read the words as they were very familiar with the story, so after the list was completed they talked together about the different sounds the letters 'ed' were making in these words.

These words all come from *Mr Gumpy's Outing*. They all end with 'ed'.

flapped	kicked	squabbled
mucked	chased	teased
bleated	trampled	tipped

Three different sounds are represented in these words by 'ed':

- 'ed' in bleated
- 't' in tipped
- 'd' in trampled

After the discussion, the teacher asked: 'Why are all these words spelt with "ed" at the end?' She was leading the children to an awareness that letter patterns may not consistently represent one sound, and that letter patterns can carry morphemic or meaning information. The 'ed' in flapped and kicked is letting the reader know that the action is in the past.

'The Ant-eater' by Roald Dahl, as well as being giggled over and perhaps read in parts, may lead to discussion of letter/sound patterns varying with accent. The following extract is taken from the poem.[14]

'Ant-eater!' he yelled. 'Don't lie there yawning!
'This is my ant! Come say good-morning!'
(some people in the USA
Have trouble with the words they say
However hard they try, they can't
Pronounce a simple word like AUNT.
Instead of AUNT, they call it ANT,
Instead of CAN'T, they call it KANT).
Roy yelled, 'Come here, you so-and-so?
'My ant would like to say hello!'
Slowly the creature raised its head.
'D'you mean that that's an ant?' it said.
'Of course!' cried Roy. 'Ant Dorothy!
'This ant is over eighty-three.'

In other words, for Australian speakers the 'au' of 'aunt' sounds like the 'ar' of 'star', but for American speakers it is like the 'a' of 'ant'. In such a discussion the children would be looking not only at the different letter-representations of the one sound (aunt, star), but also at different pronunciations of the one English spelling. They could also collect further examples of their own.

In the same way simple, familiar rhymes can be used for learning about the smaller parts of language. Some Prep children sang and clapped this little rhyme:

We are all clapping,
Clapping, clapping.
We are all clapping,
Just like this.

After it had been sung, the rhyme was displayed on a large chart; of course, the children found they could read it. They then sat in a large circle and four strips of cardboard, each with a line of the rhyme on it, were put in the middle of the circle.

Clapping, clapping.

Just like this.

We are all clapping,

We are all clapping,

First, the children arranged the strips in the correct order. Next, they were asked if they could make up a new verse to the rhyme. One child suggested 'jumping', and they all sang and jumped their way through the new verse. The teacher wrote 'jumping' on four pieces of cardboard and the children were asked if anyone could use those words to change the rhyme 'We are all clapping' to 'We are all jumping'.

jumping		jumping		Jumping		jumping

Damien volunteered, and this is what he did:

We are all | jumping |

jumping | Jumping |

We are all | jumping |

Just like this.

Sean became quite agitated as he watched Damien complete the task; at one stage he reached over and tried to move one of the cards. When Damien finished, everyone read the rhyme aloud.

'Does the rhyme make sense?'

'Yes', they all replied.

'Is everyone happy with the placement of the words?'

'No.' Sean and another child spoke. Sean got up and changed the positions of two of the cards so that 'Jumping' with a capital letter was at the start of line 2. Sean knew the term 'capital letter', as did several of the other children. (Their teacher uses it when she is demonstrating writing in front of the children.) The children talked across the circle as to why Sean moved the words — the reason being given that each line of the rhyme commenced with a capital letter. Here were children learning about capitalisation in the context of a demonstration of whole language.

With whole-language learning there is no predetermined order in which teachers must choose to have children learn about the smaller pieces of language. Language learning just does not happen that way. From the language children are exposed to — the language they see and hear around them — they will extrapolate their own understandings about how it works, and will try out these understandings. Since different children see and hear different types of language demonstrated, however, they will not all come to the same understandings at the same time. In fact, they will not all come to the same understandings.

To give just one example: each five-year-old child's name is different, so each five-year-old becomes quite familiar with the written form of his or her name, but not so familiar with the written form of other children's names. In our classrooms we see again and again that the first letters the five-year-olds use in their writing are those in their names. Therefore, the first letters learned and used by five-year-olds differ for each child.

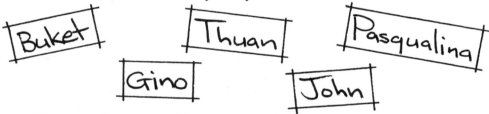

Of course, the nature of learning is such that a learner does not go from nil understanding to absolute mastery all in one lesson. From the initial immersion and modelling of some language feature, the child may try out many hypotheses or approximations as he or she moves to conventional usage. A child's spelling of 'ghost' may move from 'grbsk' to 'grS' to 'gost' to 'gosth', and finally to 'ghost' in the process of learning the conventional spelling.

Attention to skills varies with purpose and audience

It is important that authentic occasions occur as part of school programs, in which children will spend time attending to the surface features of their writing. (The surface features are spelling, punctuation and handwriting.) If, for example, children know that the book they are hand-lettering will be on display at the class book launch and that parents, teachers and other children will pick up and read the books on display, there is tremendous motivation for them to do their best possible handwriting.

An Integrated Approach to Learning

In the real world, writers vary the attention they pay to handwriting and to proofreading for spelling and punctuation in accordance with the intended purpose of — and audience for — each piece of writing. For example, we don't proofread shopping lists written for our own use, but if we write lists for other people to use we may pay more attention to our spelling, abbreviations and handwriting. We may include more information, such as brand names.

The care we take with spelling, handwriting and sentence construction in a letter to a close friend will vary in comparison with the time and care we take in drafting a letter to a parliamentary official or, for example, to the Director of Education. Children should come to be aware of this relationship between the time and care taken with writing and the intended audience.

Writing contexts in school will provide for different forms, purposes and audiences. Some of these will require fine attention to the conventions of written language, firstly by the child as writer and sometimes later with the teacher or other children acting in the editorial role; other contexts may place less emphasis on perfecting the conventions, such as when writing in a personal journal.

Authentic opportunities to handwrite well

In any classroom, during the year there are many opportunities to give children genuine purposes to practise their very best handwriting or lettering. Here are just a few.

- Designing and writing in cards for:
    birthdays (for friends or family members)
    Easter
    Christmas
    Mother's or Father's Day
    baby arrivals (for families of classmates)
    illness (get-well wishes)
    departures (farewell notes)
    engagements or weddings
- Practising a signature
- Writing letters (re excursions or local community issues, to newspapers, as thank-you notes or invitations)
- Making classroom signs, lists, captions
- Making posters
- Lettering (text) for books that are published

Any language occasion is an occasion on which the learner's attention may turn to one of the subsystems of language, and here skill learning is occurring. In an integrated learning program, where language is used for a wide range of purposes, there will be many authentic opportunities for children to proofread and edit, taking into account the purpose and form of their language and the intended audience.

Shirl and David's classroom, showing the children seated on the carpet in the whole-group meeting area

An Integrated Approach to Learning

Chapter 7 Creating the right environment

The learning environment of the classroom — and, in fact, of the whole school — gives children messages about the type of behaviour and thinking that is valued. According to its nature, the environment can either hinder or facilitate the development of thinking and creativity.

The classroom environment can be viewed as having two elements:

- the emotional/philosophical setting or context
- the physical/organisational setting

The emotional and philosophical context

Under this heading come the manifestations (overt and covert) of the teacher's and school's ideas and beliefs about a whole range of social and educational issues:

- how children learn;
- the nature of the adult–child relationship in the learning setting;
- the role of the teacher;
- how much control the teacher should exercise;
- how much say the children have;
- the nature of the teaching task;
- the place of freedom of choice for children in regard to curriculum, procedures and so on;
- the role of the adult with respect to modelling of desired behaviours, attitudes and that which is to be learned.

Your classroom climate will directly reflect how you think on such issues.

Learning involves risk-taking

We believe that learning involves risk-taking and, as a consequence, mistakes. Mistakes are a natural part of learning. It is essential that the classroom environment supports this notion in order that children may develop intellectually, explore ideas and think creatively. Yet in practice it is often the case that the classroom is a place where the children are scared to have a guess, to offer an opinion or to try something different.

'Weekly Wonders' or 'Challenge' sheets are used as a means of encouraging children to think laterally, without worrying whether their responses are right or wrong. 'Weekly Wonders' is a bit of a misnomer — the sheets actually don't appear weekly, but perhaps every three or four weeks! Mostly they are tied in with a theme or topic or a specific event, so they aren't always called 'Weekly Wonders', either! But the idea behind them remains the same. It was inspired by Virginia Ferguson's book, Twenty Tiny Textbooks.[15]

This sheet relates to a Victoria State Opera production of Beauty and the Beast, which was performed at the school.

An Integrated Approach to Learning

This sheet was related to a topic centred on 'Change'.

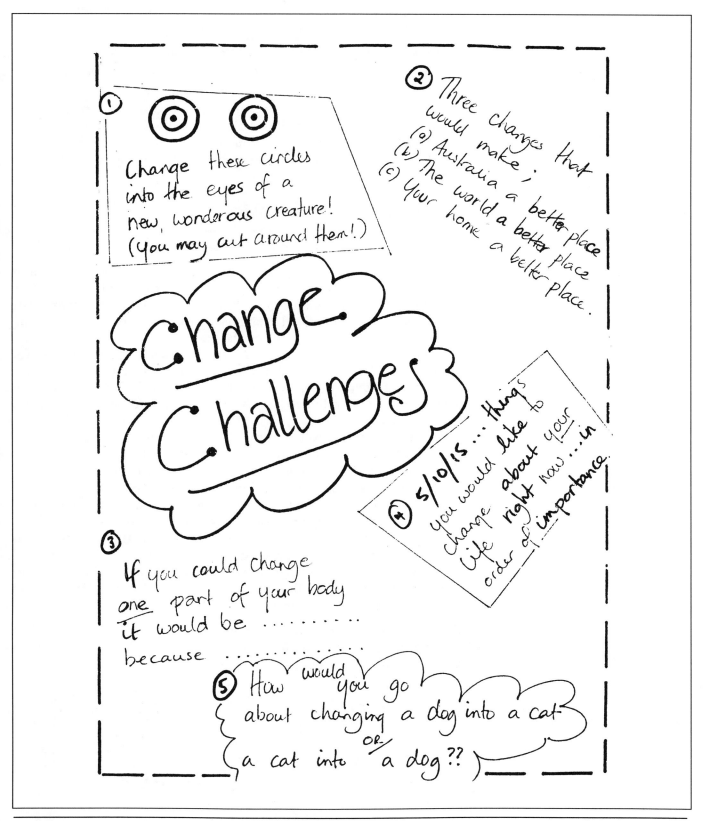

Is there a right or a wrong answer here? Are there limits to a child's response?

> *If the emphasis is always on 'getting the right answer', children will be much less likely to 'have a go', consider alternatives, guess, hypothesise and generally use divergent thinking processes.*
>
> *Integrated Curriculum Document* [16]

Do the children in your classroom respond to others' opinions and ideas with acceptance rather than ridicule? Do they encourage and help each other? Do they hear and see you accepting mistakes and encouraging the learner to try again, to try something different and to analyse why and how he or she went wrong?

Activities to develop risk taking

Use situations as they arise to practise risk-taking. For example:

1. If a new or unusual word comes up in reading or discussion, use it as an opportunity to 'have a go' at spelling it. Ask three or four children to say the word clearly and then attempt to write it on the board. The whole class can be involved in analysing the attempts, and other children will volunteer to improve on the guesses.
2. Do the same with numbers. If a large number is mentioned — for instance, 'there were 87 500 at the MCG on Saturday' — ask first if anyone will have a go at writing it on the board, and then whether someone else would like to have a try. Use the children's attempts as a basis for discussion.

   While marking the roll, you may state that 'ten out of fifty children are away today'. Invite children to consider what fraction of the class that is, to record their answer on the board and to justify it.
3. Oral reading risk-taking can be informally practised through children being asked to share in the reading of such items as newsletters, notes to be taken home and instructions or lists on the board.

   Using oral cloze while reading to the children is another way of encouraging them to take a risk, to have a guess in a non-threatening situation.
4. On excursions or trips children can be asked to make predictions; for example: 'How long it will take to walk up Athol Street? How long to go by bus to South Melbourne?'

Keep bringing the need to take risks to the children's attention when discussing things with them. Reinforce the idea by having signs, posters or mobiles around the room promoting it.

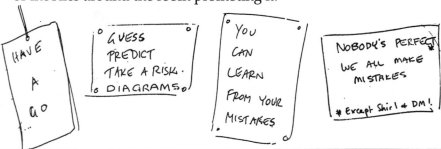

Set up formal activities (in a variety of areas) that encourage guessing and predicting.

- Spelling: Use 'Have a Go' cards
- Literature: Ask questions such as 'What do you think will happen next? Why?' 'What evidence is there to support your guess?'
- Maths: There is unlimited scope in maths for the children to be continually involved in estimating and predicting, especially in measurement activities.
  - What do you think would be the average height of people in this class? How could we find out?
  - Estimate how old you are in months, in weeks and in days. Use a calculator to check and compare your estimates.
  - Estimate how long your paces would be when walking slowly, walking quickly, jogging and running fast. Then measure and compare them.

Science involves predicting

As part of an integrated unit on 'Water', David and Shirl's children did some experiments on evaporation. They were asked to predict from which of five differently shaped containers a given amount of water would evaporate fastest, and why.

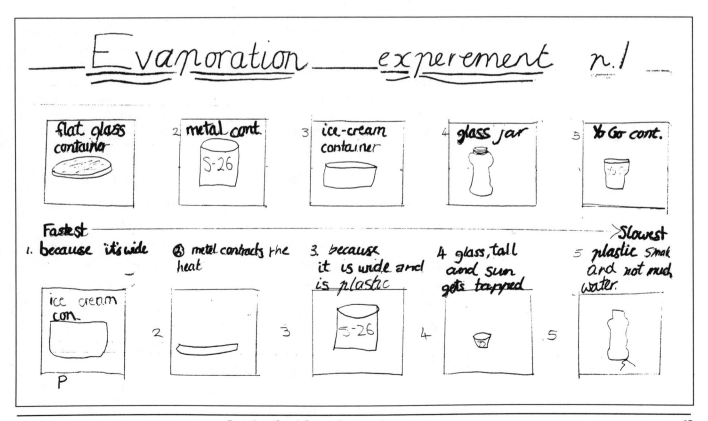

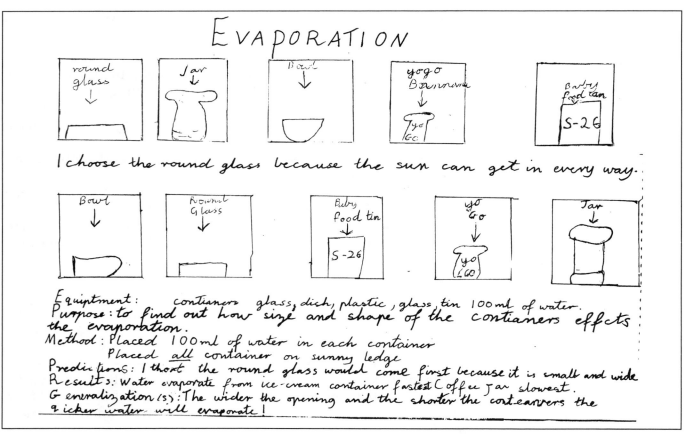

EVAPORATION

I choose the round glass because the sun can get in every way.

Equiptment: containers glass, dish, plastic , glass, tin 100ml of water.
Purpose: to find out how size and shape of the contianers effcts the evaporation.
Method: Placed 100ml of water in each container
        Placed all container on sunny ledge
Predictions: I thort the round glass would come first because it is small and wide
Results: Water evaporate from ice-cream container fastest Coffee Jar slowest.
Generalization (s): The wider the opening and the shorter the contearvers the qicker water will evaporate!

Classroom climate

We believe that the right sort of classroom climate involves honesty, trust, openness, acceptance, responsibility and self-discipline on the part of both children and teachers. This means teachers and children working together for common purposes.

It means teachers listening to children, valuing what they say, and showing that they value it. It means providing opportunities for the children to learn how to be responsible, to practise self-discipline — opportunities to choose, to plan, to do and to evaluate.

. . . the teacher does not play an authoritarian role but is rather a participant in the living and learning situation in the classroom. The teacher has the final responsibility for making decisions and setting the boundaries between what is acceptable and what is unacceptable in the room; but the discipline of the group is based on mutual respect between the teacher and the child, and between child and child, and is gradually assumed as a group responsibility. If the teacher accepts the child and the child in return has an affectionate regard for the teacher, he will begin to incorporate the teacher's values and to develop internal personal control.

M. Brown and N. Precious [16]

It means giving up much of the traditional teacher control and working side by side with children in a learning partnership. *The teacher is the role model in all respects.* It can never be a matter of 'Do as I say, not as I do'.

For the children to feel that what they say is valued, there must be established processes or structures that enable them to have input wherever possible, and that input must be acted upon.

In DM and Shirl's grade the word of the child is valued eg. we have Agenda Time. We have a list stuck up in the room. If someone wants to discuss something and wants everyone to know too, he/she puts it on the list and we argue and talk about our ideas.

ISSUES AGENDA

- FAT day (Rachael)
- Talent Quest (Pasq.)
- Assembly Comperes (Kate)
- Silent Reading (Jon)
- Camp Book (DM)

Children are free to raise any issue they like per the agenda. It is their job to speak to the grade about their concern or idea, and to invite discussion. The teachers are free to place items on the agenda. With an individual grade of twenty to twenty-eight children the discussion of issues can take place with the whole grade sitting in a circle, on chairs or on the floor. A child can chair the session. With a double grade, David and Shirl have found it necessary to organise a class committee, elected via a secret ballot. This committee meets weekly (or more frequently if required) to discuss the agenda items, and then reports back to a whole-group sharing session.

The committee members may ask questions, invite further discussion, ask for suggestions, or organise people to carry out tasks. This may lead to changes in class routines, an excursion being planned, letters being written, or discussions being held with the principal or other teachers.

Last year two of the children per the agenda suggested having a punk dress-up day. After discussing it with the committee and then with the whole grade, it was decided to have a 1950s and 1960s dress-up day instead. This then was turned into the culminating activity of a week's mini-theme on that period, which fitted into the class theme at that time — namely, 'Change'.

Children involved in program evaluation

Involving the children not only in the evaluation of their own performance but also in the evaluation of the class program is a necessary part of developing openness, responsibility and self-discipline. The children regularly evaluate aspects of the program — for example, an integrated learning unit, literature, maths, or methods of organisation. At the end of each term they complete an evaluation sheet. A sample of different children's responses is included here.

What I enjoyed at school this semester
I really enjoyed maths homework. (Michael B.)
Drama. Sport. Planning my own work. (Kate B.)
Maths because it is much different from when I did it other years. (Raegan)

What I didn't enjoy
Missing out on inter-school sport. (David E.)
The literature book '3 Cheers For 19'. It was far too easy. (Lisa P.)
Doing too many evaluations. (Kim)

What I would like to see changed
F.A.T. [Free Activity Time] in a better time — so I don't have to miss out while I'm at drums. (Aaron)
I would like to see when we have inter-schools port that we have something planned in case we don't play. (Kate B.)
Have more time to finish things. (Gayle)
Nothing. I like it the way it is. (Rebecca)

Literature
I thought literature was fairly good this term. I think it should keep going. (Max)
I enjoyed it. You got to read in your own time and at your own pace. (Lisa P.)

The children's responses are shared, discussed and taken into account in future planning.

As an aid to planning the 1989 and 1990 Grade 5–6 camps, in response to a request from David and Shirl the children carried out the following tasks.

1. Individually, they evaluated the 1988 camp.

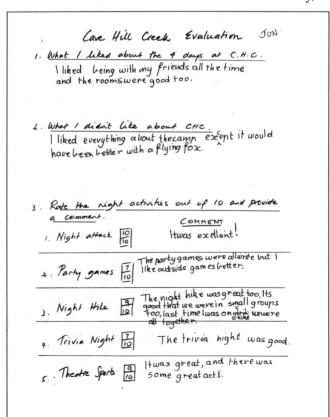

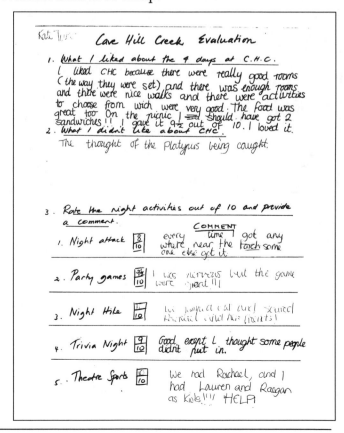

2. In small groups, they listed the things they liked or disliked about the 1988 camp and whether or not they would like to return to the venue in 1989.

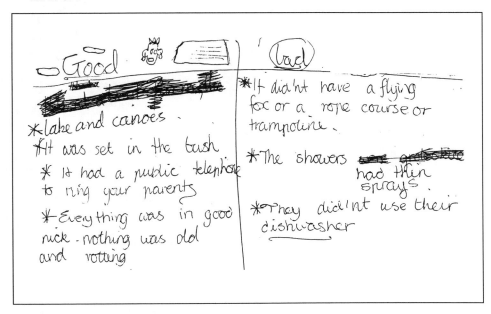

○Good (bad)

*Lake and canoes.
*It was set in the bush
* It had a public telephone to ring your parents
* Everything was in good nick - nothing was old and rotting

*It did'nt have a flying fox or a rope course or trampoline.
*The showers had thin sprays.
*They did'nt use their dishwasher

3. Finally, in groups, they came up with a list of what they considered to be the five most important criteria to be considered when planning for a camp.

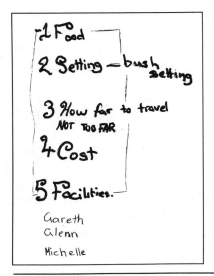

CONSIDERATIONS

1. Cost
2. Facilities. Location.
3. Rooms
4. Food
5. Facilies

1 Food
2 Setting — bush setting
3 How far to travel NOT TOO FAR
4 Cost
5 Facilities.

Gareth
Glenn
Michelle

1. The cost of the camp.
2. Setting of the camp.
3. the facilities activities that they have there.
4. how far away it is.
5. the food.

The chosen criteria were discussed and a final list compiled, ranked in order of importance to the children. The criteria were used as the basis for deciding on the venue for the 1989 camp. With respect to the 1990 camp, a small group of children were given the job of composing a letter to be forwarded to possible venues.

The replies to the letters were considered with reference to the criteria developed by the children, and this involved whole-grade discussion. Throughout this exercise the children were developing their reading, writing, oral-language and thinking abilities. Just one specific reference — writing the letter to the camp directors — involved writing for a real purpose: to collect information about possible camp venues. It was an authentic occasion on which to write in letter form, and it involved writing to unknown audiences.

Two final examples of valuing children's opinions relate to a bike hike and the Easter Hat Parade. In 1988 Grade 5–6 had its first bike hike, which involved David and the principal with fifteen or so children on each of two different days. This had its beginnings in a suggestion on the list put forward by a Grade 6 boy who had transferred from a school in the outer suburbs. They'd had a bike hike. Why couldn't we?

The children were asked to collect information about local bike tracks, bike safety, and road rules and regulations, which they did; letters were written, phone calls were made. The result was a safe, enjoyable time had by all participants at the end of the 1988 school year.

With regard to the annual Easter Hat Parade, the Grade 5–6 children have not always been noted for their enthusiastic participation. Therefore, rather than insistence that they take part, the question was put to them: 'Do you want to take part?' Small-group discussion followed, ideas were shared, and a vote was taken. The majority decision was to participate, and the responsibility for producing a worthwhile hat was then placed on each child's shoulders.

The importance and worth of listening to the children is summed up by Kellie:

> The two teachers in our grade let us have our say and value what we say ... they respect what we say and we also respect and value what they say to us.

Classroom relationships

Openness and honesty

The nature of the teacher–child relationship must necessarily be different from the traditional idea of it. It must be a relationship that is based on trust, friendship, openness and mutual respect. It means listening to and speaking with children, sharing beliefs, ideas, experiences, fears, hopes, likes and dislikes. It means being honest with oneself and with each other. We must provide the opportunities to do this and an atmosphere in which the children feel free to do it. One avenue used by many of the children is their personal journal/diary.

> Dear D.M.
> I would like to ask you a question. Why don't schools still use canes and old desks and old school rules. I think the old-fashioned ways were better ... I am in grade 6 and I will be going going out to work soon I will need discipline and to have responsibility.

This girl's entry (above) was the result of a dialogue that had been going on for sometime; it had centred around her changing attitude and behaviour and her immersion in the Madonna/Cyndi Lauper culture of the time. She rarely discussed issues in person with her teachers, but was quite ready to write pages and pages in her diary. This is a good example of the value of providing opportunity in the school writing program of writing to a known and trusted audience.

> Dear D.M.,
> Sorry for the last diary – BUT I had to let out in some old way!! NOW ... I'll tell you my personal problem. Its my parents – all they do is argue!! When they fight I feel fainting!! Thats why I'm always like this at school ... grumpy, grouchy and moody (and less friendly) ...

This child had recently transferred from a small, highly structured school. She was having trouble coping with the need to make decisions for herself and the need for self-discipline. This diary entry provided David and Shirl with a starting point for discussion with her and with her parents about ways of assisting her.

Discipline

Operating in such a classroom environment raises the issue of discipline.

With so much freedom of choice — freedom to move around, to talk, to pursue individual interests — the children need to develop the ability to make responsible decisions and, allied to that, a degree of self-discipline. These are difficult accomplishments for some children; they will not develop such abilities unless given the chance and encouragement to do so. Those who are struggling need — in this as in any learning — to be supported in their endeavours.

Taking responsibility for decisions can begin with something as simple as this:

Child: Where can I put my model to dry?

Teacher: You decide. Remember, though, we need those tables by the wall for our maths activities later.

Free activity sessions (FAT) happen on a regular basis. The children have said that they think they are valuable and consider it their right to have them. At the same time, however, they have agreed that along with this right there is the individual responsibility to keep up to date with their work. They accept the loss of their FAT if they fail to carry out their responsibilities.

The more responsible children will generally decide for themselves when they need to 'work' during FAT (some will choose to 'work' as the preferred activity in any case). Experience will show which of them need closer monitoring.

A child may ask if she can use the computer during FAT. 'Fine', we reply, 'but remember that your maths work is due tomorrow and your Yearbook by Friday. Do you think you'll have enough time?' However, although the children must be given the opportunity to learn responsibility and self-discipline, if any of them continue to take the easy way out, the teacher needs to assume more responsibility for those children's actions.

At the beginning of the week we discuss with the class the work we expect to cover during that week. A list is made, detailing what needs to be completed and when.

By looking at the general timetable for the week, the children have an idea of how they will have to pace themselves to complete the work.

This week

1. June page in yearbooks
2. Uni 'diary'. . . into yearbooks after conferencing
3. Literature
   - finish reading
   - comments
   - activity
   - wall hanging
4. FAT Day evaluations
5. Personal reports for P–T interviews
6. Class diary — illus.

	Language	S R	Maths	Art / Library		Lang.-Lit.
F A T	Maths	PE	Pers. writing	S R	← Language →	
R E	Lang. (Band)	S R	Maths	Art / Library		FAT
F A T	Personal maths	S R	Language	S R	← Language →	
F A T	Personal maths	S R	Language	← Sport →		

The children become responsible for organising themselves and for making decisions as to when they will do things. Some will need close monitoring and help in making the decisions. Others may at times need to be told what to do and when to do it. The important thing is that at least they are all given the chance to make responsible, effective decisions for themselves.

Summing up, the right environment involves giving up much of the traditional direct control being exercised by the teacher. It means allowing the children to move about freely, to talk, to take risks, to make choices, and to make responsible decisions. It requires openness and honesty on the part of the teacher and the child. It means creating a non-threatening atmosphere — one that is both accepting and challenging at the same time.

Physical and organisational context

The other important aspect of the classroom environment is the physical set-up and organisation: the furniture that is most appropriate, the furniture arrangement, materials in the room, methods of display, and storage facilities.

Decisions about the furniture and materials acquired and how they are to be arranged or distributed are a reflection of a teacher's ideas about how children learn and about his or her own role. Classroom organisation needs to reflect the following considerations.

- Children learn from each other. There need to be areas where they can work together in pairs or in small groups. Talk (working noise) is an essential element of the environment.
- Sometimes children will have individual interests to pursue. There should be quiet areas where they can do this.
- Learning takes place in a variety of situations. There must be opportunities for children to work in groups of varying size and composition.
- To provide opportunities for responsible decision making, children need to be given choices:
  - where to sit;
  - with whom;
  - what tasks to do, and when.
  Seating needs to be flexible, and the timetable needs to be accessible.
- With children working on different things at any one time (some working individually, some in groups of varying size, some talking or moving around), it means that:
  - there is no need to have a chair for each child;
  - if children are free to move and to work with different groups, they do not have a fixed work spot or chair;
  - a variety of working areas and spaces is needed;
  - time and space are needed for large-group or whole-grade sharing sessions;
  - there needs to be a variety of materials/resources readily available and accessible;
  - it is important to have a large amount of display space.

Such considerations obviously preclude an arrangement whereby there are rows of desks facing the front, the whole class work from the blackboard, and talk is discouraged or forbidden!

David and Shirl's 5-6 classroom has the following furniture, materials and spaces:

Rectangular school tables which are grouped easily.

Large kitchen-type tables with suitable chairs (used for art, science, cooking, displays).

A variety of cupboards and shelving — some fixed, some portable.

A set of six carrels for individual, quiet work.

A collection of nine or ten old armchairs, an old couch and three or four beanbags.

Large, fixed display boards at either end of the double room, plus a variety of miscellaneous ones (cane-ite boards, large sheets of cardboard, movable pinboards, mobiles).

Five trolleys for children's lockers, display and storage.

Two computers.

Paper of various sizes, colours and textures.

Variety of writing implements and illustrating material:
- Pentel pens
- calligraphy pens
- Derwents
- crayons
- charcoal
- nib pens and inks
- textas
- watercolours

Collections of books and magazines for reading (teacher- and school-bought).

Reference books for child and teacher use (art/craft, science and poetry books, dictionaries and atlases).

Miscellaneous junk (from Reverse Garbage) for art and science.

Games — simple, old-fashioned strategy games such as draughts, chess, backgammon, Chinese checkers, cards and jigsaws, plus UNO, Othello, Cluedo, Technic Lego.

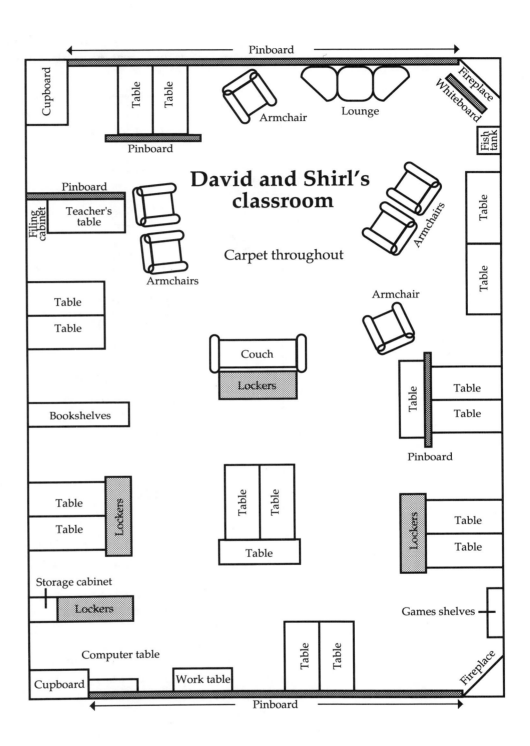

David and Shirl's classroom

Carpet throughout

Cupboard

Pinboard

Table

Table

Pinboard

Armchair

Lounge

Fireplace

Whiteboard

Fish tank

Pinboard

Filing cabinet

Teacher's table

Armchairs

Armchairs

Armchair

Table

Table

Table

Table

Bookshelves

Couch

Lockers

Table

Table

Table

Table

Pinboard

Lockers

Table

Table

Table

Lockers

Table

Table

Table

Storage cabinet

Lockers

Games shelves

Computer table

Table

Table

Fireplace

Cupboard

Work table

Pinboard

Leanne's Grade 2–3 classroom, while only a single room, has many of the same materials and areas supporting the same underlying philosophy.

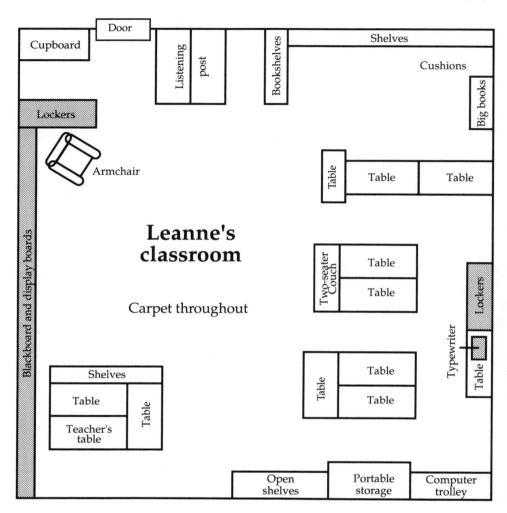

It is not, however, so much a matter of whether you have such resources that will determine the degree of success you achieve in creating a suitable environment for integrated learning; it is how you utilise what you have.

Teachers must ensure that the conditions provided are those that promote learning in an integrated way, that are at once accepting and challenging and that provide opportunities for the children to question, plan, investigate and discuss.

Chapter 8 The big problem: Classroom organisation

With the spread of the whole-language movement into schools, lots of interesting and exciting language activities are happening. A perusal of some classroom timetables reveals that language has almost taken them over, with process writing for an hour every day and process reading for an hour or more. In fact, some whole-language timetables are as tightly compartmentalised as the timetables of the 1950s.

Further perusal of these timetables shows there is little time left for a carefully developed study of the children's world. Language, maths, specialist-teacher lessons, clubs or electives leave little time in the classroom for children's ongoing involvement in an inquiry-based integrative approach.

Frank Smith says, 'The language learning is incidental, a by-product of the child's attempt to achieve some other end'.[18] This other end can be the child's self-discovery, his or her learning about community and the physical and social worlds.

Timetabling of specialist subjects such as physical education, art, music, library, community language, clubs, sport and religious education can mean that the classroom teacher is left with a collection of fragmented time-slots for language, maths and learning. This form of timetabling — that is, planning for the development of subjects — is not necessarily compatible with the way children learn.

There are also constant demands from the Ministry — and more particularly from community groups — for space in the school curriculum for yet other areas of instruction: sex education, nutrition, bike education, driver education, peace education, protective behaviours . . . the list continues to grow. The 'what' that the community wants taught has grown dramatically but the allotment of time with the children has not.

The areas of study listed above have a valid claim on our curriculum. How then do we fit them in? If we slot them into separate boxes on the timetable the boxes will of necessity become smaller and smaller, leading to further fragmentation of learning. Planning for integrated learning with units of work incorporating many disciplines is therefore a sensible alternative.

In using an integrative approach, ' . . . it is argued that children can get a much more complete picture of the topics they are investigating and become aware of the way in which the various ways of looking at a phenomenon may add to or complement each other'.[19]

The industrial issue of teacher time release has meant a necessary improvement in teacher working conditions, but where — as is generally the case – time release is provided through a range of specialist teacher lessons, such organisation is not necessarily providing better learning conditions for children. An alternative which has barely been considered is for a staff to opt not to have specialist teachers, but for each teacher to have much smaller home groups. This would permit more flexible grouping, such as two teachers working with three home groups for dance or assembly while the third teacher had time release. Such organisation would allow for much less rigid timetabling.

A small group of children work co-operatively on a given task

An Integrated Approach to Learning

Timetabling at the grass-roots level

Shirl, David and Leanne have found that planning and timetabling a program in which the children are rarely all doing the same activity at the same time — and also having to plan around specialist lessons — is a headache, and quite time-consuming. They never find enough time in the week to fit everything in. Team teaching has its own built-in problem: to find the necessary time to plan properly and in detail. Shirl and David often plan at weekends.

When planning, they first list all the activities to be considered for that week. The following is an example.

1. Activities relating to the integrated unit of work:
   (a) art — reflection pictures
   (b) drama, mime
      * an ice-block melting
      * getting into a hot bath
      * having a shower
      * in groups of 5 or 6, a tray of ice blocks is put in saucepan, gas is lit, stirred to boiling point
      * a rain dance (compose movements and put to music)
   (c) science evaporation experiments
      * shape/size of containers and evaporation rates
      * position of containers and evaporation rates
   (d) writing — directed writing experiences, Weekly Wonders sheet
   (e) word study — word-web of water words
   (f) poetry — Readers Theatre of 'The Owl and the Pussycat'

2. Other activities:
   * literature
   * personal writing
   * year books
   * share time (hobbies/ interests)
   * illustration of class books
   * FAT (Free Activity Time)
   * issues agenda — discussion, voting

When all the activities are listed, they draw up a blank timetable and fill in the weekly specialist lessons: art, library, physical education and religious education. David and Shirl timetable maths separately three times a week, and allow other time for personal maths investigations. This is not to say that much maths is not integrated. It is, where appropriate.

Silent reading is slotted in at the same time and day each week. The children then know the routine. Each morning after recess they enter quietly, get their reading material, and settle to reading quietly. The children benefit from the establishment of some routines, but the routine of the timetable must not be such that it works against learning.

The timetable at this stage looks something like this.

M.			Silent reading	Maths	Serial reading	Art / Library	
Tu.	FAT	Maths	PE		Serial reading	Art / Library	
W.	RE		Silent reading	Serial reading		Art / Library	
Th.	FAT	Personal maths	Serial reading		Serial shared reading		
F.	FAT	Maths	Silent reading		Serial shared reading		Sport

The next task is the difficult one; it is the jigsaw of trying to fit everything into the spaces and time-slots that remain. After much negotiation, the timetable could end up like this.

	10.30/10.45		12.15/1.15		2.15/2.30	
JSC to meet	**Language** • Illustrations — Daily diary / Holidays • Nit nurse writing • Hopes and fears Word study	Silent reading	**Maths**	**Art** / **Library**		**Water** • Draw and label water cycle — where does water come from and go to?
FAT	**Maths**	**PE** / Water writing • Introduce 'writer's circle'	Silent reading	**Water** • Complete water cycles • Set up terrariums • Finishees — share and discuss water cycle in small groups	**Language/Literature** D.M.:'Rebecca's World' 'How to eat fried worms' Shirl: 'My Dog Sunday' 'Bicycles Don't Fly'	
RE	**Language** • March page for year book • Personal writing D.M. 'Cybil War' / 'You remember me'	Silent and serial reading	**FAT** • Peg decorations • Silhouettes	**Art** / **Library**		**Language/Literature** D.M.:'Present takers' Shirl: 'Chocolate Touch' 'Would You Rather' • March pages • Illustrations
FAT	**Personal maths investigations**	Silent reading	**Language** • Small group share water cycles • Evaporation experiments 1. Same amount/different-shaped containers 2. Salt, sugar, dye — what's left?	Serial reading	**Water** Write up predictions and experiments • Terrariums • Water cycles	**Art** 'Reflections' / **Drama** 'Water experiences'
FAT	**Maths**	Silent reading	**Language** • March pages — year book • Write up experiments • Illustrations — Daily diary / Holidays	Serial reading	**Water** • Water page in theme book • Literature - reading - book report - activity	**Ball game practice**

Daily diary . . . . children scribe

A couple of sessions are always left open towards the end of the week and are filled in according to how the week has developed, how the activities have panned out, and which directions and tangents the children have taken.

A large copy of the timetable is displayed in the classroom for the children's reference. They can see what is to happen during the week and when it is to happen, and this makes it easier for them to organise their week's work. They often write out their own copies of the timetable, which is not permanent, nor is it followed rigidly. Each week is different, according to the school happenings, the in-class activities, the weather and so on.

Planning for two- to three-week blocks rather than for identical weeks allows for learning to flow, and not to be horribly disjointed. Teachers must stop feeling guilty about not covering everything every week. It's impossible.

Timetabling for an integrated classroom can be difficult. It is unique to each classroom. It should be a reflection of the teacher's philosophy of education — of how the teacher believes children learn — as well as a reflection of the school program and a response to the needs and interests of the children.

Creating a co-operative learning environment

As an integrated curriculum involves children working together, consideration must be given as to how to establish a co-operative learning environment. Generally speaking, it does not just happen. Certain strategies and methods need to be employed to foster a caring, cohesive group of children who can work co-operatively. The following strategies may be useful in helping to establish such an environment.

- If the children are not accustomed to working together, it could be quite chaotic initially. It may be easier to start by getting them to work in pairs for certain activities and then gradually provide opportunities for them to work in groups of three or four.

  If the first few attempts at group work do not succeed, persevere.
- It is often a good idea to elect (or to let the children decide on) members of the group to assume certain roles: for example a scribe, a timer, an encourager, a reporter and a reader. This helps to keep the children on task and makes sure that all members of the group are involved.
- It is important to discuss elements of co-operative group work with the children before, during and after activities. While they are working in groups it is essential to circulate among them, modelling effective co-operative behaviour. Make comments, for example, such as 'That's a good idea', 'What do you mean by that?' or 'What do you think?'
- After group work, it is very useful to select a member from each group to report on how successfully they worked, what didn't work and why, and anything that might be changed for the next time. If the children expect to be given the opportunity to reflect upon their group's behaviour and the members' contributions, they tend to work harder to achieve effective results.

Small Group Evaluation.

Group Members : _____
_____ _____
_____ _____

	Poor	O.K.	Good
Our group co-operation			
Our work effort			
Our finished product			

We are happy _____
_____
_____

Next time we could try _____
_____
_____

Individual Group Member's Evaluation.

NAME : _____   DATE: _____

I listened to others. ☺ 😐 ☹

Others listened to me. ☺ 😐 ☹

I waited my turn ☺ 😐 ☹

I worked well with others ☺ 😐 ☹

I kept my mind on the job. ☺ 😐 ☹

- As a class it is extremely useful, after many experiences of working in groups, to compile a class list of the particular behaviours that enable groups to work co-operatively and effectively.

  Leanne's grade came up with these important group behaviours:
  - to sit where everyone can see the task, or the paper being used to record on (for instance, in a circle);
  - to listen to others;
  - to keep on task at all times;
  - to include all members of the group;
  - to accept others' suggestions without making fun of them;
  - to help each other.

  This list is displayed in the room and is often referred to before, during and after group work.

- Different group combinations should be trialled to give the children a variety of experiences in working co-operatively. Sometimes they can be given the choice of who they want to work with (friendship groups), but at other times certain combinations may be insisted upon — for example, having mixed abilities or mixed social skills within a group, placing a child who needs encouragement with another who is caring and understanding, or placing an effective leader within each group.

- Our school community has developed a discipline policy which is also useful in enhancing co-operative group learning. It is based upon the children being aware of their rights and responsibilities and the rights and responsibilities of others.

  In each class, at the commencement of a new year, the children discuss these concepts and establish a list of rights and responsibilities appropriate to themselves. These are displayed for all to see (opposite page).

  If a child fails to respect the rights of others or shirks his or her responsibility, the matter may be discussed either with the child individually or, if appropriate, with the entire class. Action will always be a logical consequence. For example, a child found scribbling on a table may have to spend some free time cleaning it off.

Having a consistent approach to discipline throughout the school assists in creating effective co-operative learning environments within the classrooms, as the children are aware of the expectations and have learned to respect the rights of their classmates.

Creating a co-operative learning environment may not be an easy task, but it is a necessary component of learning through an integrated curriculum. It is essential to take the time and effort to establish such behaviours within the classroom by providing as many opportunities as possible for children to experience learning in groups and by allowing time for discussion and reflection upon their efforts.

RIGHTS	RESPONSIBILITIES
In this room — you have the right	and the responsibility ....
• to be listened to	• to listen to others without fiddling, making noises or talking over them.
• to work in a room that's not too noisy	• to work quietly without disturbing others.
• for your opinion to be respected & to make your own decisions	• to listen to other's opinions & not make fun of them.
• to have some of Leanne's time	• to not interrupt people when they are spending time with Leanne.
• to use equipment in the room	• to share the equipment
• to work in a clean room	• to pack up your mess and look after the room.
• to move freely within the classroom (within reason)	• to be considerate of other people when moving.
• for your time not to be wasted	• to line up quickly, come in & sit down quietly and stop and listen when asked to
• for your property to be safe in the classroom	• to take care of other people's property & not touch something that isn't yours.

An Integrated Approach to Learning

APPENDIX 1:
Integrated learning units

A topic may be taken with children of different levels and be educationally valuable to all because each integrated learning unit begins with the children's existing understandings and knowledge, and develops along different paths according to different interests. To illustrate this point Leanne, David and Shirl chose to plan units on 'Water', which they then developed with their respective grades, 2–3 and 5–6.

Unit 1:
Water (Leanne's Grade 2–3)

Focus question 1: What are the properties of water?

Contributing questions
1. How can water change?
2. When does water change?
3. How can we make water change?
4. What floats/sinks in water?

Focus question 2: Why is water important to us?

Contributing questions
1. What do we need/use water for?
2. Who needs water?
3. How much water do we use? How much do we need?
4. How do people/animals adapt to water shortage?
5. How can we conserve water?
6. How is water polluted?

Knowledge

Understandings
Water can be a solid, a liquid, or a gas. It can change from one state to another.

There is a natural water cycle.

Some things become buoyant in water.

People, animals and plants depend upon water for survival.

People waste and pollute water.

We need and use water in many ways.

Concepts
Buoyancy
Evaporation
Condensation
Gas, liquid, solid
Conservation

An Integrated Approach to Learning

Facts
- About the water cycle
- Related to concepts

Skills

Critical thinking
Questioning; hypothesising; generalising; critically examining and evaluating data; suggesting consequences; speculating about the future.

Social interaction
Working co-operatively and constructively with others; being tolerant of others; accepting criticism and advice.

Communication
Participating in group discussions; expressing understandings clearly and effectively; recording results; producing written, oral, drama displays.

Research
Observing; experimenting; predicting; interpreting results; gathering, organising and classifying data.

Values

- Valuing water: concern about waste and pollution
- Appreciating water as an essential element for the preservation of life

Action

Display book of experiments.
Advertise with posters, e.g. 'Turn the taps off'.

Initial activities

Before the commencement of the unit, the children were asked to form groups of three or four and to write down all the things they knew about water. Each child had a role as recorder, reporter, encourager, or the person to keep the group on task.

Leanne wrote all the groups' statements on a large piece of paper; then, as a class, they tried to group the statements together. This took a lot of questioning and directing. They decided on a name for each group; examples were 'animals and water', 'uses of water', 'water sports', 'water changes' and 'food and water'.

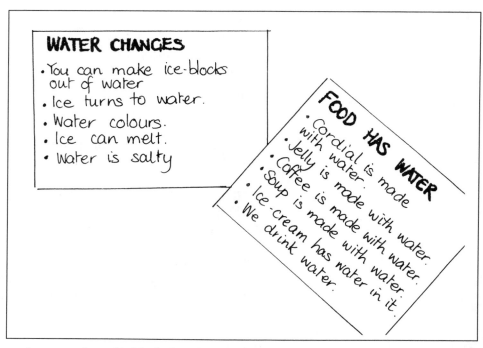

Leanne then divided the children again into groups in order to list all the things they would like to find out about water.

WHAT DO WE WANT TO FIND OUT?

* WHERE DOES WATER COME FROM?

* WHERE DOES WATER GO TO ?

* HOW DOES WATER EVAPORATE ?

* HOW DOES WATER COME FROM THE SKY ?

* HOW DO YOU MAKE JELLY ?

* HOW DO YOU MAKE WATER

* HOW DO YOU MAKE ICE-CREAM ?

* HOW DOES WATER DISAPPEAR ?

* HOW DO WE FLOAT ?

* HOW DOES PLASTIC FLOAT ?

* HOW DO TREE TRUNKS FLOAT ?

* HOW DO WE GET CLOUDS ?

* WHERE DOES WATER COME FROM WHEN WE SWEAT ?

* HOW DOES WATER GET TO A TAP ?

* HOW DOES WATER GET FROM ONE PLACE TO ANOTHER ?

An Integrated Approach to Learning

After discussions with the children, two areas of focus were chosen around which to develop an integrated unit of work. These were:

- What are the properties of water?
- Why is water important to us?

All the children's statements were displayed around the room and were continually added to, changed and reflected upon throughout the unit of work. These statements were also used by Leanne and the children to evaluate the unit.

Focus 1: What are the properties of water?

Inquiry	Related activities

Evaporation

Acquaintance activity
Go outside and talk about what will happen when water is poured onto the asphalt. Pour water, and draw around outline with chalk. What is happening? Check at regular intervals, then discuss what happened to the water.

As a class, write up the experiment.

Gathering information 1
Set up an experiment in the classroom. Cut off the top of a balloon. Place the balloon on top of a jar half-filled with water. Mark the water line, then place the jar in the sun.
   Make predictions. Observe what happens throughout the day. Discuss why the balloon fills with air.

Set up terrariums, using plastic coke bottles.
Graph growth. Record daily observations.

Set up an experiment to test what affects the rate of evaporation. Place jars filled with the same amount of water:
- outside in the sun
- outside in the shade
- inside in the sun
- inside in the cupboard
Make predictions. Check results regularly. Make statements.

Organising information
Write up experiments as a grade. Make a big book of experiments with illustrations by children.

Working in pairs, describe what it would be like if it didn't rain for a year and all the water was just evaporating. Draw a picture of what the ocean would look like if all the water was gone.

CONTENTS

EVAPORATION RATE

Purpose: to find out whether water evaporates quicker inside in a cupboard or outside in the sun.

Equipment needed:
2 jars

Method:
Put the same amount of water into two jars. Mark the water line on both jars. Place one inside in the sunlight and the other in the cupboard.   p. 4.

Predictions:
Some people thought the water in the cupboard would evaporate quicker while other people thought the water in the sunlight would.

Results:
After 1 day: the jar placed in the sunlight had evaporated more than the jar in the cupboard.

After 1 week: A greater amount of water had evaporated from the jar in the sun compared with the jar in the cupboard.   p.5

Gathering information 2
Put a pot of water to boil, having first measured the amount. Let it boil rapidly for 15 min. Place a plastic sheet above the pot; observe condensation on the plastic. Let the water cool, then measure the amount. Compare this with what was put in.
• Predict what will occur.

Why isn't our water salty? Dissolve some salt in a small amount of water. Pour some of this into a container with a large surface area and let it evaporate.
• Note the results.

Write up the experiments as a class. Add to the big book of experiments.

Drawing together
In small groups, make statements about evaporation and the water cycle. Display the statements.

Refer to initial questions: 'What did we want to find out?' Have any of the questions been answered?

Focus 1: What are the properties of water?

Inquiry	Related activities

Buoyancy

Gathering information

In groups of three or four, conduct experiments on activity cards. Topics are:

- floating and sinking
- making things float and sink
- making floaters to float in salt water, fresh water, oil and milk; comparing buoyancy
- making jars sink by adding water
- making modelling clay float

Record group results and report to the class.

Working in pairs, design and construct a boat that will float. Have boat races. Discuss why certain boats went faster than others.

Volume activities:
1. Experiment with a tub of water and containers, ordering capacities of containers from least to greatest. 2. Use one container to see how many times it will fill other different containers. Tally.

Discuss and use measurement — millilitres and litres.

Read *Who Sank the Boat?* by Pamela Allen.[20] Discuss illustrations; note the water line.

Working in small groups with a 'boat' and a number of objects, find five objects which together will just sink the boat. Record the order in which they are put in the boat. Does the order matter?

Read *Mr Archimedes' Bath* by Pamela Allen.[21] Experiment with plastic animals.

Freezing

Gathering information

As a class or in small groups, first predict the result of this experiment. Pour water into a container. Mark the level of water, freeze it, then mark the level of ice. Compare this with the first mark.

- Has anything happened?

Draw what was done, and what happened.

Do the same with:

- dirty water
- salt water
- water and cordial
- milk

Pretend that it is so hot that the familiar things about you have started to melt. Draw what some things would look like, e.g. your house, your pencil, a bicycle.

Using thermometers, find out which school drinking tap gives the coolest water.

Focus 1: What are the properties of water?

Inquiry	Related activities
Use an ice-block and a clear glass container to discover whether more of the 'iceberg' floats above or below the water. Draw a diagram to show what you found.	In pairs, write a description of water for a robot with no human senses (sight, smell, taste, feel or hearing). Incorporate what you have learnt about evaporation, freezing, buoyancy.

Use an ice-block and a clear glass container to discover whether more of the 'iceberg' floats above or below the water. Draw a diagram to show what you found.

What will happen to 'icebergs' if placed in three different sorts of water?
- hot water
- salt water
- water with detergent

Write up experiments in big-book format.

In small groups, write statements about freezing.

Drawing together
Present your big book of experiments to another grade.

As a class, refer to the chart listing 'Things we want to find out about water'. Mark off those which were found out; reflect upon other things you found out (refer to statements made throughout investigations), and discuss whether there is anything else you would like to find out.

                              and/or

Evaluate:
- What I learnt about water
- What I found interesting
- Any other comments

Related activities

In pairs, write a description of water for a robot with no human senses (sight, smell, taste, feel or hearing). Incorporate what you have learnt about evaporation, freezing, buoyancy.
or
Conversational writing: one person is the robot, another is any character he or she chooses. Have a conversation about water.

Role-play this to the whole grade.

Focus 2: Why is water important to us?

Inquiry

Acquaintance activity
In pairs, look through magazines and cut out all the pictures that show people using water. Group the pictures. Discuss the groupings as a class.

Use the letters of the word 'water' to create a display, e.g.

WATER

Stick the pictures onto the letters. Make statements below each letter related to the different uses of water.

Gathering information
List all the times you or your family use water during one day. Graph results. Make statements.

In small groups or as a class, design a survey to ask your family and friends about the importance of water. Sample questions are:
- What are the five main things you use water for?
- Have you ever been to another country where the water supply was different from ours? How was it different?
- If you had to reduce your water usage, what would you cut down on?

Related activities

Water rhymes: Form groups of four. From a selection of poetry related to water, each group is given a different poem, divided into four parts. You are given these instructions:
1. Leader reads to group, others follow along.
2. All read together.
3. Leader allots parts.
4. Practise in parts.
5. Decide on actions.
6. Perform to grade.

Read *Lester and Clyde*.[22] Hold a 'press conference' (see Appendix 2).

Focus 2: Why is water important to us?

Inquiry	Related activities

In small groups, list the five most important uses of water, in order of priority. Compare group decisions (each group must justify their decisions). Try to come to an agreement. *(Values activity)*

- Three of the class are interviewed as Lester, Clyde, and the 'Man'.
- Remaining class members all write down two questions to ask each of the characters (questions that are not answered in the text).
- The three 'characters' prepare to be interviewed by discussing what they may be asked.

Role-play:
- a discussion between Lester and Clyde about the polluted pond;
- a discussion between Lester and a person who was polluting the pond.

Discuss your experiences of polluted creeks, rivers, beaches, etc.
- What happens as a result of all this pollution?

Add to statements answering the question: 'Why is water important to us?'

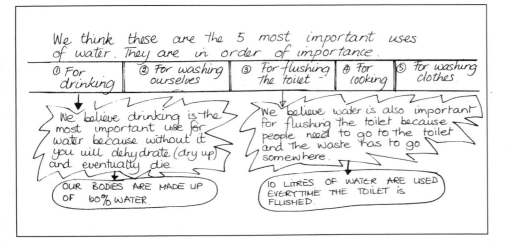

Look at pictures or videos of how people in other countries use water, e.g. in a country where the one river is used for washing clothes, cooking, drinking (including by animals), bathing, going to the toilet.

In small groups, list all the ways in which people waste water. Divide into pairs, each pair making a collage showing one of the ways water is wasted.
- What could happen if people keep on wasting it?
Combine collages and display them.

Drawing together
You have been shipwrecked on a deserted island with a group of people. There is no fresh-water supply. You have 10 litres of water to last you two weeks, until the next ship sails by. Calculate how much water you would go through daily, and for what uses. *(Values activity)*

Focus 2: Why is water important to us?

Inquiry	Related activities

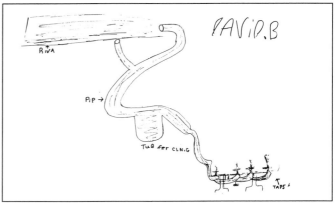

Illustrate your idea of how water gets to the taps. Discuss predictions. Find out the answer.

Each write statements:
> Water is . . .
> As wet as . . .
> When it rains, I . . .
> Swimming is . . .

Make class books, using the above statements. Design pages using water paints, straw-blowing, finger painting, sponge painting.

In small groups, list how life would have to change if water didn't come from taps and a water tank was your only supply. Relate to the position of people who live in the country.

Discuss why we shouldn't waste water and how we can stop people from wasting it, e.g. place posters around the school: 'Turn off taps'. (*Action component*)

Create a certain number of rules that will help all families to conserve water. (*Action component*)

Refer to initial questions: 'What do we want to find out about water?' Go through the questions to see if you now know the answers.

Discuss how you would tell others the things you have learned about the importance of water; e.g. make little booklets to distribute to others; write a small play to perform to others; re-enact the story of Lester and Clyde. (*Action component*)

Unit 2:
Water (David and Shirl's Grade 5–6)

Focus question 1: Where does water come from?

Contributing questions
1. How do clouds form and produce rain?
2. Why does it rain?
3. How are hail and snow formed?
4. Where does water go after it rains and after we've used it?

Focus question 2: What properties do the various states of water have?

Contributing questions
1. At what temperature does water freeze and boil?
2. How does water differ from one state to another?
3. Where does water occur naturally in each of its states?

Focus question 3: Is water an unlimited resource?

Contributing questions
1. How is our drinking water made clean?
2. How is water misused or wasted in homes?
3. How much of the world's water supply can we use for drinking?
4. What are the causes of water pollution and what can be done about it?

Focus question 4: Is water essential to all life?

Contributing questions
1. How many litres of water do we need in order to function?
2. How do animals, plants and we ourselves adapt to the availability of water?

Knowledge

Understandings
There is a water cycle.

All water comes from a process of evaporation and precipitation.

Water occurs naturally as a solid, a liquid or a gas.

Solids:
• expand when frozen;
• will float (e.g. icebergs);
• need space (ice).

Liquids:
• support the weight of objects;
• refract light;
• have surface tension.

Gas:
• rises when hot, condenses when cool;
• is present even though it cannot be seen.

Most of the world's drinkable (potable) water is either salty or in the form of ice.

Man has polluted the little drinkable water we have.

People waste water unnecessarily.

Differences in the distribution of water affect the environment and lifestyles of animals, plants and people.

All living creatures need water to survive.

All living things contain water in their body cells in varying degrees.

Concepts
Evaporation
Pollution
Conservation
Water as essential to life
Scarcity of water

Facts
- About the water cycle
- About the three states of water
- Concerning distribution of water in the environment
- On availability of potable water
- About household consumption

Skills

Critical thinking
Brainstorming; predicting/hypothesising; analysing/interpreting; speculating; observing.

Social interaction
Group work (working co-operatively); combining in drama groups.

Communication
Discussion; sharing experiences; writing and recording clearly; debating.

Research
Experimenting; problem solving; collecting data; observing; reading.

Values

- Recognising the need to conserve water, a scarce resource

Action
Display posters (designed by children) around school as reminders to turn taps off.

Emphasise the need for children themselves to make a concerted effort to turn taps off at home and at school.

Encourage children to talk to those in other grades.

Arrange for children to write letters to relevant people — to parents, through the Newsletter; to the local council regarding the state of Queen's Park, Moonee Ponds Creek and the Maribyrnong River.

Acquaintance activities

1. Brainstorm in a large group on the topic 'Water'; write results up as a flow chart, showing all possible areas of investigation.
2. In pairs, children list knowledge/statements of understanding, and questions they'd like answered. Collate (working in large groups). Display statements and questions.

GR. 5/6 (WATER QUESTIONS)

Was the world once covered in ice? Will it occur again?

What causes bubbles?

How do fish get to be in water?

Why is sea water salty?

Why does it rain?

How is snow, hail formed? What causes tides?

How clean is our drinking water?

What is actually underneath islands?

Where does water come from?

What's the biggest recorded flood in Q.L.D.?

How many litres of water are drunk by adults, chn. at M.P.W. each week, each hot week?

How much water do we use at home in a week?

How do mozzies breed in water?

At what temp. does water- freeze, evaporate?

How do clouds produce rain?

Why do people need water?

How does air pressure keep water out of diving bells?

How long can a person survive w/out water?

---

3. Small groups classify or group statements and questions.
4. Children individually draw and label diagrams of where they think water comes from, how it gets to a house, where it goes to — the children's version of the water cycle.

   In small groups, children share their versions. Other children question or comment.

An Integrated Approach to Learning

Focus 1: Where does water come from?

Inquiry	Related activities

Gathering and organising information
Write to Melbourne & Metropolitan Board of Works for information about excursion to sewerage farm.

Set up terrariums.
- Predict what will happen.
- Observe.
- Record findings.
- Share results with class.
- Hypothesise why terrariums do/don't dry out.

Evaporation experiments:
1. Shape/size of container in relation to rate of evaporation
   - Predict what will happen.
   - Record results.
   - Share findings with class.
   - Make generalisations.
   - Model writing up an experiment.
2. Position of container in relation to rate of evaporation (e.g. sunny outside, sunny inside, dark inside, dark outside, shaded inside)
   - Predict results.
   - Record results.
   - Write up the experiment in a theme book.

Read the story 'Skeleton on the Dunny', in Paul Jennings' book, *Unreal*.[23]

Make reflection pictures using watercolour paints.

Word study: Brainstorm 'water' words. Write out lists for display.

Think/talk/write about 'Have you ever...?'
- desperately wanted a drink;
- plunged into water fully clothed;
- slept on a waterbed;
- been frightened by water;
- run out of water;
- eased yourself into a really hot bath;
- been caught in a down-pour and drenched;
- seen a flood;
- nearly drowned;
- splashed through puddles in the rain;
- plunged into freezing-cold water;
- had your skin become wrinkled like a prune.

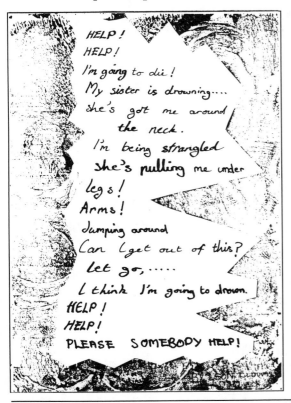

Focus 1: Where does water come from?

Inquiry	Related activities
Cloud formation experiment: In small groups, attempt to make 'clouds', following a given instruction card. Prepare a diagrammatic explanation of how clouds form and why a cloud 'rains'. In small groups, conduct experiments to find what is left after various water solutions (using salt, sugar, food dye) have evaporated. • Predict and record results individually. • Share results with others. List the sources of drinking water. Invite a speaker to address the grade (e.g. a plumber or a representative from MMBW). • Brainstorm and list specific questions to ask the speaker. • Write a letter to the appropriate person if no speaker is available. Redraw a diagram of the water cycle. Build a dam in a sandpit. Investigate for the best site, how to prevent seepage, the need for strong retaining walls. Construct channels for water flow. *Drawing together* In small groups read the sheet on the water cycle in the booklet from MMBW. Present four or five statements about what is learned from the article. Share the statements with others.	Research an area of individual interest, answering a question raised in brainstorming. Read and share water poem: 'Water', by Michael Rosen.[24] Drama: In groups of five or six, make up a rain dance; invent both movements and music.

Focus 2: What properties do the various states of water have?

Inquiry	Related activities
Acquaintance activity Observing water: Work through the following activity individually or in pairs. 1. Fill a container (clear) with water. Touch the surface with one finger, then slowly pull the finger away. What happens to the surface? Does it rise, fall or stay the same? Draw the shape you see just before your finger leaves the water. 2. With the container at eye-level, look through the water at objects placed behind it. What do you notice? Be prepared to discuss your results. 3. Put a spoon, a pencil or a straw into the container so that the object is half-submerged. What do you notice. Draw what you see. Then place the container at eye-level. Does the object look the same?	Use oil paints and water to create marbling. Make pictures by blow-painting.

An Integrated Approach to Learning

Focus 2: What properties do the various states of water have?

Inquiry	Related activities

4. Hold a drop of water on the end of a straw; let it fall onto a piece of chinagraph plastic.
   - What shape is the drop? Look closely. Try another drop. Is it similar?
   - Put a drop of water over a printed word. What do you notice?
   - Which of these shapes is closest to the shape of your drop? Draw the shapes. ⌒⌒ ⌒⌒⌒ ⌒⌒
5. Sprinkle some pepper or some powder paint onto the surface of the water. Touch the surface with a piece of soap. What happens? Be prepared to discuss what you see.
6. Drop an object into a large container of water. Draw the pattern the ripples make. Is it ◎ or ((·)) or ◎ ?
Share findings and experiences. Make generalisations.

Water as a liquid

Gathering and organising information
1. Buoyancy
   - Plasticine boat experiment:
     Using 50 g plasticine, make a boat that will float. Load it with plastic beads. How many will it carry before sinking?
   - Egg experiment:
     Place one egg in a jar of fresh water, another in a jar of salty water. Predict what will happen. Observe, and make generalisations.
2. Surface tension
   - Fill a glass with water to 'overfull'. Observe and draw what you see.
   - Find a way to float a pin or a needle. Observe and draw what you see. Add detergent to the water. What happens? Make generalisations.
   - Float four matches in a star shape on water. Rub some soap on the end of a straw; dip the straw into the water in the centre of the matches. Observe what happens. Make generalisations.
3. Refraction
   - Observe objects in water. Draw and record your observations.
4. Displacement
   - Using 50 g plasticine, form various shapes. Experiment to discover which shape displaces the most water. Make generalisations.

Read *Mr Archimedes' Bath* and *Who Sank the Boat?*

Research the topic in relation to submarines.

Water as a solid (ice)

Gathering and organising information
Ice needs space — water expands when frozen.
- Fill bottles with water, seal with foil caps and place in freezer. Predict what will happen. Record results. Generalise.
- Fill drinking cups with water, marking the level before putting in freezer. Predict what will happen. Record results.

Look for information on the *Titanic*.

Using coloured ice-blocks, discover which colour melts fastest. (*Chalkface*, August 1986.[25])

Focus 2: What properties do the various states of water have?

Inquiry	Related activities

Water becomes lighter when frozen.
- At what temperature does water freeze? Try measuring with a thermometer; when water starts to ice up, record the temperature.
- Which freezes faster — hot or cold water? Devise and conduct an experiment to find the answer. Record and write up findings.
- What substances affect the rate of freezing? Try adding colouring, salt, sugar, detergent or milk, or using dirty water. Record and write up experiments. Make generalisations.

Problem solving: Try to keep an ice-block from melting, using anything you like.

Water as a gas (steam/vapour)

Gathering and organising information
Observe the temperature at which water boils.

Vapour forms drops as it condenses.
- Put ice-blocks in a glass jar and observe drops forming.
          or
- Put a glass jar in the refrigerator. Observe what happens over time. Draw what you see.

Drawing together
Use drama sessions to demonstrate one or more of the points raised; for example:
  Water expands when frozen.
  Water makes objects buoyant.
  Water has surface tension.

Draw up a list of generalisations about the properties of water.
Make this into a book, and illustrate it.

Focus 3: Is water an unlimited resource?

Inquiry	Related activities

Acquaintance activity
How many litres of water do you use? Look at a litre of water.
- Predict your consumption using shower, bath, toilet, washing machine, dishwasher, sprinkler and hose, and when cleaning teeth, washing hands, drinking.

ITEM	GUESS	ACTUAL
Shower		
Bath		
Toilet		
Hose		
Teeth		
Drinking		

Search newspapers for any references to water — e.g. usage or pollution.

Write to MMBW or the Conservation Council asking for someone to come and talk about the need to conserve water.

Focus 3: Is water an unlimited resource?

Inquiry	Related activities

Compare predictions with actual figures (obtainable from MMBW). Make a chart, as illustrated.
 	
Investigate actual consumption. Discuss ways of recording, e.g. noting water meters over two days, on weekdays, at weekends, and averaging the figures.
 	
Gathering and organising information
In groups, list appliances and fittings for which water is needed. Circle the three that use the most water.
 	
Predict the percentage of water used in an average household in:
    kitchen
    laundry
    bathroom
    garden
    toilet
    other places
If possible, give actual figures.
	Investigation: Highlight difficulties of obtaining water in countries where it is not on tap in the household. Physically fill and carry buckets a given distance (e.g. 100 metres). Work out how many trips would be needed and how much time would be spent collecting water for your family.

In groups of five or six, discuss why we might need to curtail water use. • How many reasons can you think of for the need to use less water? Discuss this in a large group. How could we curtail our own water consumption? • In pairs, list the ways your households could reasonably save water. Share and discuss ideas as a large group. Draw a graph comparing monthly rainfall with water consumption! • What does it tell us? • What assumptions can we make?	Investigation: Work out how much water is wasted by taps dripping or not turned off at school. Give factual information. • A dripping tap wastes 47 000 litres of water a year.

Drawing together
Suppose that Melbourne has had a dry winter and spring. The reservoirs are not holding much water because the rain did not arrive, and Melbourne is facing a serious water shortage. There will be a summer drought. Work in groups to eliminate three water uses in order to save water. Justify your choices. *(Values activity)*

Devise slogans and/or posters to be displayed around the school, encouraging everyone to turn taps off. *(Action component)*

Write an article for your newsletter; plan a message for parents. *(Action component)*

Focus 4: Is water essential to all life?

Inquiry	Related activities

Acquaintance activity
Select objects such as types of food or soil.
- Weigh them.
- Let them dehydrate
- Weigh them again.

What objects in the environment contain water?
Which of them would contain the greatest proportion?
Predict the percentage.

Small group investigation:
'Our body is 80% water'.
- How big a puddle would you make if you melted?

Gathering and organising information
Experiment: How much water do plants need? Select various plants which you then water:

daily
weekly
not at all
only when soil is drying out

Observe and record results.

Try the same experiment using cacti watered daily, weekly, or not at all. Observe and record results. Generalise.

Talk about hunger strikes.
- How long can people survive without water?

Survival activity
In small groups, list ways of surviving in a remote area.
What would your priorities be?
How long could you go without (a) water and (b) food?

Drawing together
Write factual statements about:
- the properties of water;
- the water cycle;
- how much water is in the world;
- how important water is to life.

Working in pairs or small groups, share these statements, check them for accuracy, delete duplicates, group those that belong together, then sequence. Present this pooled information to the grade, orally or in written form.

You are stranded in the Sahara Desert with the following people: a healthy expectant mother, a retired gentleman, a terminally ill person, a fit and able man, a young child, a doctor, a nun, a criminal and a famous entertainer. There is only enough food and water for five people to survive.
- Who will survive? Why? (Values activity)

Focus 4: Is water essential to all life?

Inquiry	Related activities

Debate whether a new reservoir should be built, even if this would mean flooding a valuable and beautiful piece of land close to Melbourne and causing many people to lose their homes. List pros and cons.
(Values activity)

Drama (grand finale to unit): In a large group (about 20 to 25), represent the stages of the water cycle using movement and music instruments.

Unit 3:
Australian Aborigines (Leanne's Grade 3–4)

The Australian bicentenary provided the impetus for this unit of work.

Focus question 1: How was the lifestyle of the Aborigines before European settlement different from our way of life now?

Contributing questions
1. What food did they eat?
2. How did they procure their food?
3. What type of shelters did they have?
4. How was Aboriginal life guided by the Dreamtime stories?

Focus question 2: How has the Aborigines' way of life changed since European settlement?

Contributing questions
1. Have Aboriginal food requirements changed?
2. How have European customs affected Aboriginal homes?
3. Are the Dreamtime stories still important to Aborigines?
4. Have all Aborigines been affected by European settlement?

Knowledge

Understandings

White people have not always lived in Australia.

The Aborigines' way of life changed when Europeans settled in Australia.

Not everyone has the same sort of lifestyle.

There are disputes between Aborigines and Europeans today.

Concepts
Culture
Tradition
Religion/beliefs
Prejudice
Lifestyle

Facts
- Regarding the lifestyle of different Aboriginal tribes
  - religion
  - food
  - clothing

Skills

Critical thinking
Listing; grouping and classifying; analysing; decision making; problem solving; comparing and contrasting.

Social interaction
Working co-operatively; tolerating others' points of view.

Communication
Reporting; role-playing; oral presentation; reading; listening.

Research
Observing and analysing slides; reading books and newspaper articles.

Values

- Respect for the Aborigines' culture
- Empathy and respect for the Aborigines' feelings about the bicentennial celebrations
- Acceptances of different cultures

Action

Groups report to the whole grade about their research.

Display the Weekly Challenge for the whole school to see. Share Weekly Challenges of different grades. (The Weekly Challenge is a task given to the children to be completed within the week. This particular task was to construct a traditional Aboriginal shelter using natural materials.)

Visitors
Invite a representative from an Aboriginal group to talk about traditional beliefs and customs.

Invite an Aboriginal dance group to the school.

Focus 1: How was the lifestyle of the Aborigines before European settlement different from our way of life now?

Inquiry	Related activities
Acquaintance activity Working in groups, list what you know about Aborigines. In pairs, list all that you would like to find out about Aborigines. Display the questions and discuss ways in which they could be grouped, e.g. by asking 'How do these questions have something in common: What do Aborigines eat? Where do they get their food?' What headings can be used to group the questions? • As a class, make suggestions such as Food, Shelter, Clothing, Entertainment, Children, Weapons, Aborigines today, Daily activities. Form small groups , each group selecting a topic heading and picking out all the questions relevant to it. Add to the list if possible. Share the work between groups, and discuss as a class. *Gathering information* Listen to and read Dreamtime stories. Write down what you know about Dreamtime stories, adding to, deleting or refining original statements. Write your own Dreamtime stories.	List four things you may have thought or done if you had been an Aborigine when the Europeans arrived. *(Values)* List four things you may have thought or done if you had been a European settler seeing Aborigines for the first time. Share your thoughts with a friend. *(Values)* Role-play situations arising between two Aborigines, two Europeans, and Europeans and Aborigines. *(Values)*

Focus 1: How was the lifestyle of the Aborigines before European settlement different from our way of life now?

Inquiry

Related activities

Listen to Dreamtime stories on tape.

Re-enact the stories.

Act out 'stories from the Dreamtime'.

Art: Put Dreamtime stories in picture form; divide them into the main parts and illustrate each one.

```
HOW THE PENGUIN GOT TO BE BLACK.
              A dreamtime story, written by Sallie Flynn.
One night in dreamtime when wishes came true, a white penguin
was walking on the beachside when it began to rain.
He said, "I wish the rain would change colour. It's always white,
that's why I'm white."
Just then the rain stopped.
SUDDENLY it started again but this time it was black.
"Oh Ah," said the penguin and tumbled on his stomach.
His body was all black now, head to toe except for his stomach
which was white.
"I think I have learnt my lesson. From now on, I am not going
to wish for anything unless it's food, off course."
```

```
HOW THE CLOUDS GOT SO WHITE.

                            A dreamtime story, written by
                                            Gayle Patterson.
Back in the dreamtime the first clouds were always black.
One day a little girl was walking around her camp.
Her father was mixing white paint.
The little girl bumped her father and white paint went
everywhere.
A big gust of wind came and blew the paint up to the black
clouds.
It went all over the clouds. They turned pure white.
"You silly girl, you wasted my white paint," said her
father.
"I'm sorry dad, I didn't mean to do it."
So thats how the clouds got to be so white.
```

Look at the type of food Aborigines ate and how they got it.

Discuss with others what you had for breakfast, lunch and tea. List and draw a typical daily diet, e.g.:
    Breakfast: Toast, cereal, orange juice
    Morning play: Biscuits
    Afternoon tea:.......
    Tea:.......
In groups of three or four, compare and contrast diets.

As a class, discuss where all this food comes from. Make generalisations; e.g. 'My food comes from Mum. Mum gets it at the supermarket. The supermarket gets it from factories and farms.'
    Display this information as a menu, showing What? Where? How?

In groups of three or four, suggest the type of food you think Aborigines previously ate and where they got it from.
- Share suggestions among groups.
- Display suggestions.

Focus 1: How was the lifestyle of the Aborigines before European settlement different from our way of life now?

Inquiry	Related activities
Using books, pictures or slides, research in pairs what the Aborigines ate, where they got it and how they got it.	Maths: Discuss how the Aborigines measured time.

Using books, pictures or slides, research in pairs what the Aborigines ate, where they got it and how they got it.
* Present the information as a chart:

What!	Where!	How!

* Compare this information with suggestions and initial statements.
* Discuss why Aboriginal food was different from ours.

Using the headings suggested before, make statements as a class about the topics. Refer to p.105.

In small groups, suggest what types of religious beliefs, entertainment and so on the Aborigines may have had.

In pairs, research one topic and present your findings to the class (answering the questions originally devised).

Compare the findings with your predictions.

Display the results.

Watch an Aboriginal dance group.

Drawing together
Draw a picture of the three things you would have liked best about living as the Aborigines used to.

Draw a picture of the three things you like best about the way you live. Share your pictures with the class.

Role play: An Aboriginal child from 200 years ago discusses with you how you could spend the day together.

Refer to the questions you listed at the beginning of the unit. Discuss all you have learned so far.

Related activities

Maths: Discuss how the Aborigines measured time.

Trace shadows on asphalt; check and retrace at regular intervals throughout the day.

Make models of the type of housing Aborigines had.

Prepare food they may have used, e.g. grind wheat or bulbs.

Make models of Aboriginal cooking implements.

Create 'Aboriginal' paintings and carvings.

After seeing the dance group perform, write different sorts of poetry, e.g.:
Acrostic poem

Beating sticks
Over and over
Only
Men
Elders watching
Really exciting
Acting like
Native animals
Great performance!

Play some Aboriginal games, e.g. 'rhythm sticks'.

Dance: Imitate Aboriginal movement and music.

Tell stories through movement and mime.

Focus 2: How has the Aborigines' way of life changed since European settlement?

Inquiry	Related activities

Acquaintance activity
Conversational writing: In pairs, imagine you are convicts coming to Australia.

Make up a written 'conversation' with your partner.

Gathering and organising information
Press conference: Use the book, *Joe Nangan's Dreaming*.[26] Read excerpts from the introduction — 'The Source of the Legends'. Choose class members to represent characters from the story:
- Aboriginal mother or father
- Aboriginal child
- Two white people

All prepare two questions to ask each of these four people, e.g.:

How did you feel when . . . ?

What did you do when . . . ?

Imagine that an Aboriginal child comes to school and some children are picking on him or her because the child won't join in the school bicentennial celebrations.
- List two things you could do to help the other children understand.
- List two things you could do to help the Aboriginal child feel more welcome.

Analyse and reflect upon the information that you have found in your research throughout this unit. Consider these questions:
1. Do the Aborigines still live like this?
2. Where in Australia do Aborigines still retain elements of traditional lifestyle?
3. How do other Aborigines live?
4. Why has their lifestyle changed?

In small groups, work out alternative ways of presenting the information, e.g. in murals, models or books.

Drawing together
Refine the initial statements.

Reflect upon whether the initial questions were answered.

Share work with other grades and perform role plays selected from those that were done as part of the unit.

Unit 4:
The body (David and Shirl's Grade 5–6)

This unit was undertaken because the children requested it.

Focus question 1: What are the major components of our body?

Contributing questions
1. What are the special features of the major parts?
2. What are the interrelationships of these organs?

Focus question 2: How and why do peoples' bodies change over time?

Contributing questions
1. What are the effects of the ageing process?
2. How can disease change our bodies?

Knowledge

Understandings
Each part of the body has a specific function.

The body is a system of interdependent parts.

A balance of rest, exercise and food is needed for the system to function properly.

Some people are born with bodies out of balance.

Diseases such as cancer can cause unnatural changes in bodies.

The body changes and develops over time.

Concepts
Physical development
Ageing
Abilities and disabilities
Nutrition

Facts
- About functions of
  - the heart/blood/circulatory system
  - the eyes
  - the digestive tract
- Relating to the effects of a proper or improper diet

Skills

Critical thinking
Questioning; listing/grouping; brainstorming; suggesting consequences.

Social interaction
Working in groups — working co-operatively.

Communication
Participation in group discussions; presenting understandings (written and oral) clearly and effectively; role play.

Research
Observing; predicting; gathering; organising and classifying data from books, pictures, reading sheets, interviews and models of the human body.

Values

- Recognising the need to look after our bodies, taking exercise and watching diet
- Acceptance that
  - everyone is different
  - people have different abilities

Action

Make changes to improve diets.

Excursions/Visitors
Visit 'The Everybody Exhibitions' at Incinerator Theatre, Moonee Ponds.

Invite a speaker to talk about being blind and or deaf.

Invite speakers to talk about special diets and allergies.

Invite a doctor, a nurse or a community health person to chat with children.

Focus 1: What are the major components of our bodies?

Inquiry	Related activities
Acquaintance activity Draw and label diagrams of bodies — their insides and their outsides. Display the drawings.	In groups, check the correct spelling of body parts.

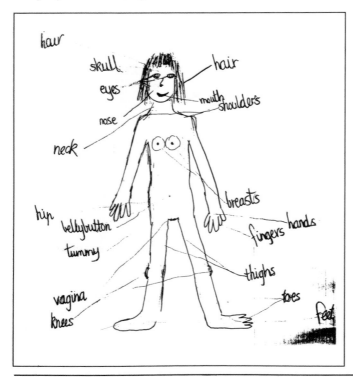

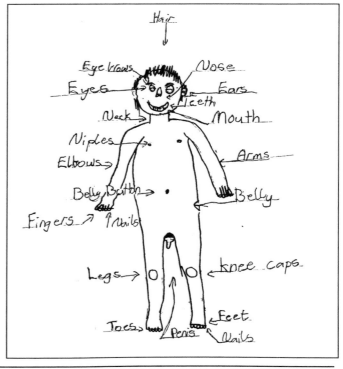

Focus 1: What are the major components of our bodies?

Inquiry	Related activities
In pairs, write down statements of your existing knowledge about the body. Collate and display them.	Trace a diagram of the male/female body from an enlarged overhead projection. Label the diagram and display it.

In pairs, write down statements of your existing knowledge about the body. Collate and display them.

Make a list of things you would like to find out about. Group your questions in categories and display them.

The heart

Gathering and organising information
Draw a diagram of the heart as you think of it. Make predictions about its size, colour and shape.
  Put the diagrams into project books.

Draw an outline of the body. In it sketch the heart, marking its connections to any other parts of the body and organs you know of.
  Share in small groups.

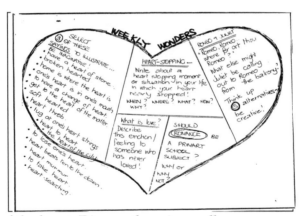

Look at models or diagrams of the heart. Discuss them in small groups.

Examine pulse rates:
• at rest;
• after walking;
• immediately after exercise;
• after 3 or 4 minutes' rest.
Record and graph results. Make generalisations. Display the information in theme books.

In groups of three or four, dissect ox or sheep hearts.
• Draw the heart before and after dissection.
• Look for parts already mentioned in discussion.
• Write up process in a theme book, describing:
  what you used;
  what you did;
  what you felt about it;
  anything you learnt/discovered.

Related activities (right column):

Trace a diagram of the male/female body from an enlarged overhead projection. Label the diagram and display it.

Investigation (MCTP lesson): Examine the relationship between body characteristics, e.g. height and armspan, height and size of feet.

Weekly Wonder sheet: The heart.

Make your own personal records. Include data such as:
• weight
• height
• handspan
• longest finger
• widest smile
• circumference of head or stomach
• reach of arms

Read *The Guinness Book of Records*[27] to extract information about the body.
• Compare these with your own performances.
• Discuss.
• Display conclusions by labelling a body outline.

In groups, discuss the pros and cons of organ donation.

Argumentative writing: 'Blood donation should be a compulsory community responsibility and service'.

Focus 1: What are the major components of our body?

Inquiry	Related activities

Drawing together
Review initial statements and questions about the heart; change and reword wherever appropriate.

Drama: In large groups (six or seven), represent a working model of the heart.

The digestive tract

Gathering information
Children read the story 'Diary of an Eaten Hamburger'[28] which details what happens to the hamburger and where it goes after it's been eaten.

Visit The Everybody Exhibitions'; study and listen to the model of the digestive tract and its noises.

Drawing together
Drama: As a large group (20/25), represent a working model of the digestive tract, including:
- food (processing)
- noises
- motions
- parts

Haiku poetry:
'Hear the churning tubes
Rumbling and noisy gurgles
A glorious belch!'

Model the various parts of the digestive tract out of play dough. Fit them into a life-size paper cut-out body.

The eyes

Acquaintance activity
Draw and write what you know about eyes.

Gathering and organising information
In pairs, set up a number of simple experiments to find out about:
- optical illusions;
- blind spots;
- pupil size in bright or dull light;
- moving two fingers back and forwards;
- putting index finger onto object at arm's length;
- left or right eye dominance;
- walking blindfold along a straight line.

Write up findings from experiments; share and discuss as a large group.

While blindfold:
- Write your name in the centre of a sheet.
- Find your locker.
- Play 'bammyknocker', 'farmyard animals', 'walk the plank', 'blindfold soccer'.

Listen to a guest speaker talking about being blind.

Dissect a sheep's eye.
- Predict shape, texture, feel.
- Draw the external view.

After dissecting, discuss what you found. Write a brief account of your findings.

Suppose you had the choice between not being able to see and not being able to hear.
- Which would you choose? Give reasons for your decisions after considering the effects of each disability.

MCTP lesson: 'Portraits'.

Examine a camera lens and relate it to the way our eyes work.

Make 'flick cartoon' book.

Investigation: Which are the worst and the best colours of chalk or textas to use on the blackboard or on paper?

Survey: How many children wear glasses?
- male
- female

Focus 1: What are the major components of our body?

Inquiry	Related activities

Inquiry

How do the following animals see?
- a bat
- an owl
- a cat

In groups, select one of these to research.

Drawing together
Write about what it would be like to be blind.
- What would you find difficult?
- What would you miss a lot?

Related activities

How many people watch TV for more than two hours a day?

Weekly Wonder sheet: Eyes.

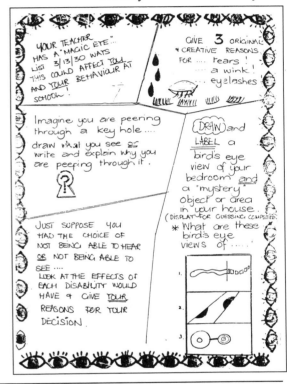

Focus 2: How and why do peoples' bodies change over time?

Inquiry	Related activities

Inquiry

Acquaintance activity
Look through magazines for as many faces of differing ages as possible. Group them in categories and make into a mural.

Draw a diagram of your body. List the differences you would find in it as a baby, at present, and as an old person.

Related activities

Investigation: 'The body area is $2/3$ of the height measurement squared.' In groups, work out how true this statement is, using newspaper, tapes and pins.

Rogues gallery: Bring in baby photos and have a guessing competition.

Investigation: Is age related to size (circumference) of head?

Focus 2: How and why do peoples' bodies change over time?

Inquiry	Related activities
	Jokes: Make a book or chart of 'body' jokes and puns, e.g. 'What do you call a man with a car on his head? JACK!!!'

Word web: Draw up lists under the following headings:
- Upper and lower body parts
- Voluntary and involuntary movements
- Inside and outside parts

Example:

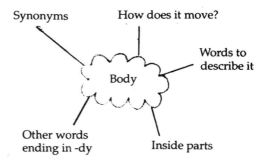

Make a similar web with individual body parts.

Gathering and organising information

Diets: Keep a record of what you eat over a period of time (3 days).

　Discuss, analyse, compare and contrast. Make value judgments on what should be changed in individual diets.

Ask a person from a fitness or a footy club to come and talk about:
- training
- diets
- exercise

Body alphabet:

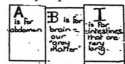

A is for abdomen
B is for brain — our "grey matter'
I is for intestines that are very long.

Focus 2: How and why do peoples' bodies change over time?

Inquiry	Related activities
	Take a plastic bag. Put into it samples of everything you eat or drink in one day — get an idea of just *how much* is eaten in a day.
	Discuss, as a large group, the problems of anorexia nervosa, bulimia, and the social pressures on people today.
Visit 'The Everybody Exhibitions'. Study the life-size models of: the children the pregnant lady grandma grandpa father baby Discuss. Study the nutrition display.	Symmetry pictures: Cut large pictures of faces from magazines. Cut each one in half and paste it on a sheet of paper.
	Finish the picture by putting in the appropriate details.
	Imagine that some part of your body has been moved to a new position. Work out the problems/advantages.
Drawing together Working in groups, list in order what you would least like to do without: sight, hearing, arms, legs or speech. Give reasons for selections.	Drama: In groups of six or seven, choose something to do with the body, e.g. the function of a particular organ or system. 'Perform' it, in mime, 'play' or song.
	Imagine the body as a machine. Give three brief instructions on the care of various body parts.

Appendix 2: Strategy lessons

Written conversations

Two children write a conversation with one another. They may write either as themselves, or as two characters from a news event or a story (for instance, Cinderella and the Prince). They share one large piece of paper, writing with different-coloured textas.

They begin by writing their names on either side of the paper, at the top. Writing in different colours makes it easier for them to read back their conversations.

Sally	Brooke
Who's going to your party?	
You, Megan, Jane, Kate, Melissa.	
What food are you having?	
Party pies, sausage rolls, jelly cakes and an ice-cream cake. Are you coming?	

Sometimes they themselves may select their partners; sometimes the teacher pairs an experienced writer with a less experienced one, as this is a great modelling activity.

When the conversation is finished, the two children proofread together.

Readers Theatre

In small groups, children rehearse the reading of a text which later they will read to the whole grade. The group size equals the number of speaking parts in the text.

It may be a poem, a rhyme, a story or a play, but it must be suitable for part-reading.

There should be either multiple copies of the text or a copy in big-book form, ensuring that all group members can see it.

Each group has a leader. The leader has two cue cards prepared by the teacher: one is a set of directions; one is a list of characters.

Card 1
Readers Theatre
1. Allot parts.
2. Practise in parts.
3. Present reading to everybody.
(For a group where all members can read the text)

or

Readers Theatre
1. Leader reads aloud.
2. All read together.
3. Leader reads aloud.
4. Allot parts.
5. Practise in parts.
6. Present reading to everybody.
(For a group where some children may not at first be able to read the text)

Card 2
Hattie and the Fox
1. Narrator
2. Hattie
3. Sheep
4. Goose
5. Pig
6. Horse
7. Cow
The Readers Theatre group can work quite independently of the teacher.

Press conference

Either the teacher reads a text aloud or the children all read the same text individually. Beforehand, the children are advised that following the reading they will be attending a 'press conference' with the main characters from the text.

After the reading, children are asked to volunteer to represent the main characters of the story. The rest of the grade play the members of the press gallery.

The 'members of the press' all list two or three questions which they wish to ask the guests at the press conference, while the 'characters' try to predict the questions they will be asked, and practise some answers.

When all the questions are prepared, the press conference proceeds.

Letter-diaries

Each child shares with the teacher an exercise book in which they write letters to one another. Each aims to write once a week. The letter-diary is the confidential property of the teacher and the child, and is not read by others unless both agree.

This is a splendid way for teacher and child to become better acquainted. As well, it is a great way for the teacher as an experienced writer to give feedback about the child's spelling, punctuation and capitalisation by using in reply some of the child's words and phrases.

Argumentative language

Children work in groups of three or four, each assuming a role: reader/scribe, checker or reporter.

Using a large sheet of paper so that all group members can see, the scribe lists the group's arguments for and against a given statement, e.g. 'Smoking should be banned'. The statement to be discussed may be selected by either the teacher or the children.

After 20 minutes of listing the arguments, all children move into one large circle. The circle may be chaired by either the teacher or a child. The chairperson's role is to:

- ask a reporter to report an argument;
- invite speakers to speak for or against the argument;
- encourage quiet children to contribute;
- repress domineering speakers.

This procedure is then repeated, with other reporters being invited to present their arguments.

Optional follow-up
Later the children may write their individual points of view on the topic discussed, or in a general sense summarise the key arguments for and against.

An Integrated Approach to Learning

References

1 Goodman, K. 1986. What's Whole in Whole Language? Portsmouth, NH: Heinemann, p. 30.
2 Lovitt, C. & D. Clarke. 1988. Mathematics Curriculum and Teaching Program Professional Development Package, Activity Bank, vol. 1. Canberra: Development Centre.
3 Cambourne, B. 1988. The Whole Story: Natural Learning and the Acquisition of Literacy in the Classroom. Gosford, NSW: Ashton Scholastic, p. 36.
4 Tough, J. 1976. Listening to Children Talking. London: Ward Lock Educational, p. 80.
5 Smith, F. 1986. Writing and the Writer. Hillsdale, NJ: L. Erlbaum.
6 ———. 1988. Insult to Intelligence: The Bureaucratic Invasion of Our Classrooms. Portsmouth, NH: Heinemann.
7 The Primary School Curriculum: A Manual for Schools. 1979. Victoria: Education Department (Publications Branch), p. 32.
8 The Social Education Framework P–10. 1987. Victoria: Ministry of Education (Schools Division).
9 Based on models in the following publications:
  Johnson, P., K. Pigdon, G. Poynter & M. Woolley. 1980. "Developing integrated units for social studies: a planning model." Mansoc (Journal of VASST). 5 (1): 6.
10 Cambourne, B. 1987. "The turning tide: The move towards whole language approaches to literacy education." Literacy Eureka. Ballarat: Conference Proceedings. Sept.
11 ibid.
12 Fox, M. 1988. Hattie and the Fox. New York: Macmillan.
13 Burningham, John. 1990. Mr. Gumpy's Outing. New York: Henry Holt.
14 Dahl, R. 1986. "The Ant-eater." Dirty Beasts. New York: Puffin.
15 Ferguson, V. & P. Viska. 1984. Twenty Tiny Textbooks: Creative Writing in a Matchbox. Victoria: Hodja.
16 Integrated Curriculum Document. 1986. Victoria: Ministry of Education (Schools Division), p. 26.
17 Brown, M. & N. Precious. 1970. The Integrated Day in the Primary School. London: Ward Lock Educational, p. 26.
18 Smith, F. 1988. Insult to Intelligence: The Bureaucratic Invasion of Our Schools. Portsmouth, NH: Heinemann.
19 The Primary School Curriculum, p. 32.
20 Allen, P. 1990. Who Sank the Boat? New York: Putnam.
21 ———. 1991. Mr Archimedes' Bath. New York: HarperCollins.
22 Reece, J. 1976. Lester and Clyde. Gosford, NSW: Ashton Scholastic.
23 Jennings, P. 1991. "Skeleton on the Dunny." Unreal! New York: Viking.
24 Rosen, M. 1986. "Water." DON'T Put Mustard in the Custard. North Pomfret, VT: Trafalgar.
25 Chalkface. 1986. Melbourne: Curriculum Branch, Ministry of Education (Schools Division), GPO Box 4367. 6:4 (August).

26 Nangan, J. & H. Edwards. 1976. Joe Nangan's Dreaming. Melbourne: Thomas Nelson.

27 McWhirter, N., ed. The Guinness Book of World Records. New York: Bantam.

28 Gilmour, A. & N. Hitchcock. 1985. "Diary of an Eaten Hamburger." Health and Education: Mind and Body. Melbourne: Longman Cheshire.